HEAVENLY Cakes

JOANNA FARROW

★

JACQUI HINE

PREMIER
EDITIONS

NOTES ON USING THE RECIPES
For all recipes, quantities are given in metric, Imperial
and cup measurements. Follow one set of measures
only as they are not interchangeable. Standard 5ml
teaspoons (tsp) and 15ml tablespoons (tbsp) are used.
Australian readers, whose tablespoons measure 20ml,
should adjust quantities accordingly. All spoon measures
are assumed to be level unless otherwise stated.
Ovens should be pre-heated to specified temperature.
Microwave oven timings are based on a 650 watt output.
Eggs are a standard size 3 unless otherwise stated.
Where chocolate squares are listed in ingredient lists,
this applies to American readers.

Published in 1993 by Merehurst Limited,
Ferry House, 51-57 Lacy Road, Putney, London SW15 1PR

Copyright © Merehurst Limited 1993

ISBN 1 897730 04 7

A catalogue record of this book is available from
the British Library

Edited by Katie Swallow and Jenni Fleetwood
Designed by Maggie Aldred
Photography by Clive Streeter and James Duncan
Typesetting by Litho Link Limited, Welshpool, Wales
Colour Separation by Fotographics Ltd, UK-Hong Kong
Printed in Hong Kong by Wing King Tong

The material in this book also appears in *Simple Cakes* and
Chocolate in the Sugarcraft Skills Series.

CONTENTS

★

✦ INTRODUCTION ✦

Heavenly Cakes is a sumptuous collection of no less than twenty-two mouthwatering cake recipes. Ranging from traditional tea-time favourites like fondant-iced Petits Fours, Rich Chocolate Fudge Cake and meringue-frosted Coffee and Walnut Cake to more elaborate treats like the truffle-filled White Chocolate Box, novelty Clown Cake and Easter Nest decorated with marzipan chicks, there is a cake to suit every taste and occasion.

All the cakes are based on the introductory section of the book. This illustrates in step-by-step detail a whole host of cake, icing and frosting recipes. This enables even the most novice and inexperienced cook to achieve highly professional results. And if preferred, the basic recipes can be used on their own, or combined with other recipes to create truly individual results.

The section on Chocolate Decorations is guaranteed to prove a source of motivation. Instructions are given for making a selection of impressive decorations such as caraque, cutouts and boxes and chocolate leaves. The recipe for Modelling Chocolate is sure to inspire you to turn your hand to following the step-by-step instructions for making the most stunning chocolate rose decorations.

If time is short, you will be glad to know that most of the basic cakes in this book can be baked in advance and stored in the freezer. This enables the cook to complete the decoration at a later time, if wished. In fact, Madeira cakes and American sponges actually improve if made a day or two in advance. Whisked sponges, however, are best eaten on the day of baking.

The key to successful baking lies in the accurate measuring of ingredients. Metric, imperial and cup measures are given for ingredients in this book. Take care to follow one set of measures only as they are not interchangeable. Be sure to use the correct size and shape cake tin, too; remember that a round tin is smaller than a similar square one.

✴ LINING CAKE TINS ✴

Little is needed by way of special equipment to make the cakes in this book. Most of the items listed below will be found in the average kitchen, although you may wish to invest in a few more icing tubes (tips) and a sugar (candy) thermometer. It is a good idea to reserve a sieve, rolling pin and a couple of new wooden spoons exclusively for baking.

Cake Tins (Pans) Most of the cakes in this book are cooked in two shallow tins rather than one deep tin. Choose rigid tins with straight sides, and measure across the bottom.

Bowls Large glass or china bowls are best for mixing. Since they are heatproof they can be placed over hot water and can be thoroughly cleaned; essential when whisking egg whites.

Spoons Use measuring spoons for accurate measuring of small amounts. A large metal spoon is essential for folding in dry ingredients. Wooden spoons are used for beating and creaming mixtures, and for stirring ingredients in a saucepan.

Knives A small sharp knife is useful for cutting round templates. Use a large palette knife for spreading icing over the top of cakes, and a small one for coating the sides. For cutting cakes, a serrated knife is most successful.

Whisks/Mixers Use a metal balloon whisk for whipping cream or whisking egg whites. These allow the maximum amount of air to be incorporated while leaving a hand free for adding other ingredients. Electric mixers are useful, particularly for one-stage cakes.

Sieves A fine metal sieve should be kept exclusively for sifting dry ingredients.

Paper/Card Tracing paper and thin card are required for templates. Use greaseproof or non-stick paper (parchment) for lining tins (pans) and good quality parchment for making piping bags.

Piping Tubes (Tips) Much of the piping in this book is done using a plain piping bag fitted with a medium writing tube. A ribbon tube would also be useful.

1 **Square, Rectangular and Swiss Roll Tins (Jelly Roll Pans)** Place tin on greaseproof paper (parchment) and draw around base. Cut around shape, leaving a 5cm (2 in) margin all round for a deep tin; a 2.5cm (1 in) margin for a shallow tin. Cut in from corners.

2 Brush base and sides of tin (pan) with melted vegetable fat (shortening), place paper in tin and brush it into position. The cut paper at the corners should overlap. Brush paper lightly with vegetable fat and dust with flour, see step 3.

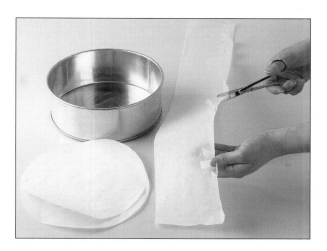

1 **Deep Round and Square Tins (Pans)** Cut two circles/squares to fit base. Cut a piece of paper long enough to go around the tin and 5cm (2 in) deeper. Make a 2.5cm (1 in) fold along length of paper; snip at intervals between edge of paper and fold.

Round Tins (Pans) Shallow tins are base lined only. Place tin on paper, draw around the base and cut out circle. Brush melted vegetable fat (shortening) over base and sides of tin and position paper circle. Brush with fat. Sprinkle a little flour into tin to coat evenly.

2 Brush side and base of tin (pan) with melted vegetable fat (shortening). Place one of the prepared circles/squares on base. Brush prepared paper strip into position around side of tin, with snipped edge lying flat on base. Put in second circle/square of paper; brush with melted fat.

Ring Tin (Tube Pan) Draw around base of tin as though there were no hole in the middle. Cut out circle, fold in half and cut out hole slightly larger than the centre of the tin. Brush tin base and walls with melted vegetable fat (shortening). Fit paper into base of tin.

Basic Recipes

★

This chapter shows how to make the basic cakes, toppings and fillings that are used in the following chapters. There are foolproof recipes for such classic cakes as Victoria sponge and Madeira cake, and toppings such as marzipan, buttercream and chocolate fudge icing. Clear, step-by-step photographs and easy-to-follow instructions accompany each recipe, ensuring that even the novice cake-maker will be able to bake a perfect cake.

Victoria Sandwich Cake

Preheat oven, prepare tins (pans) (see pages 6-7) and set out ingredients. The quantities below are for two 20cm (8 in) round layers or an 18cm (7 in) square cake.

★

185g (6 oz) butter, softened
185g (6 oz/³⁄₄ cup) caster (superfine) sugar
3 eggs, beaten
185g (6 oz/1¹⁄₂ cups) self-raising flour

★

FLAVOURINGS
Chocolate Substitute 30g (1 oz/¹⁄₄ cup) flour with cocoa (unsweetened cocoa powder).
Coffee Add 3 tsp instant coffee with flour.
Citrus Add grated rind of 1 lemon or orange.

2 Add a little egg at a time, beating hard between each addition, until mixture has slackened, then add remaining egg a little more quickly. If eggs are cold or added too quickly, the mixture may curdle. If this happens, add 1-2 tbsp flour.

1 Preheat oven to 190°C (375°F/Gas 5). Beat butter and sugar together in a bowl. When ready, mixture will be pale in colour and light and fluffy in consistency. Grated citrus rind may be added at this stage.

3 Sift half the flour into the bowl with coffee or cocoa, if using. Fold gently into mixture, using a large metal spoon. Cut through to the bottom of the bowl employing a figure-of-eight action to blend flour through mixture. Repeat with remaining flour. Do not overmix.

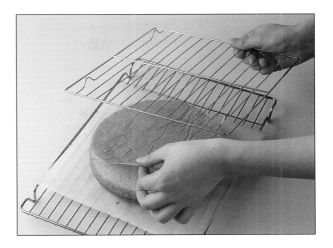

4 Scrape mixture into prepared cake tins (pans). Spread out evenly. Level surface of mixture with the back of a metal spoon, taking care not to pack the mixture down too firmly.

6 Put a piece of greaseproof paper (parchment) on top of the cake and invert a wire rack on top. Turn cake out, peel off paper and then replace it. Using a second rack, repeat process to turn the cake right way up. Remove paper; and leave cake to cool. Repeat with second cake.

5 Place cake tins (pans) on a shelf just above the centre of the oven. Bake 3-egg mixture for 20-25 minutes; 4-egg mixture for 25-30 minutes. When cooked, cakes will be golden in colour all over and the top will spring back when gently pressed with fingers.

Quick Mix Sponge

The mixture below is for two 20cm (8 in) round cakes. For a 4-egg mixture increase all ingredients by one-third.

185g (6 oz) soft margarine
185g (6 oz/³⁄₄ cup) caster (superfine) sugar
3 eggs, beaten
185g (6 oz/1¹⁄₂ cups) self-raising flour
1 tsp baking powder

Preheat oven to 180°C (350°F/Gas 4). Prepare tins (see pages 6-7). Beat ingredients for 2-3 minutes until combined. Spoon into tins and bake for 25-30 minutes until firm to touch.

Genoese Sponge

Before preparing mixture, preheat oven and prepare tins (pans) (see pages 6-7). The quantities below are for two 18cm (7 in) round layers. For two 20cm (8 in) round layers or an 18cm (7 in) square cake, increase sugar to 125g (4 oz/½ cup), eggs to 4, flour to 125g (4 oz/1 cup) and butter to 60g (2 oz). For two 23cm (9 in) round layers or a 20cm (8 in) square cake, increase sugar to 185g (6 oz/¾ cup), eggs to 6, flour to 185g (6 oz/1½ cups) and butter to 90g (3 oz).

★

3 eggs
90g (3 oz/⅓ cup) caster (superfine) sugar
90g (3 oz/¾ cup) plain (all-purpose) flour
flavourings, below
45g (1½ oz) butter, melted

2 Sift flour and any dry flavourings onto a sheet of greaseproof paper (parchment). Sift again over the surface of the mixture. Drizzle the warm butter into the bowl. Gently fold in to ensure that all flour has been incorporated.

1 Preheat oven to 180°C (350°F/Gas 4). Combine sugar and eggs in a heatproof bowl. Whisk over hot water until mixture is very thick, pale and creamy. When whisk is lifted, its trail should be visible on the surface of the mixture for a few seconds. Remove bowl from heat.

3 Divide mixture between prepared tins (pans), gently tapping the sides to level the mixture into the corners. Bake at once. A 3- and 4-egg mixture will require 15-20 minutes; a 6-egg mixture 20-25 minutes.

Swiss Roll

Preheat oven and prepare tin (pan), (see pages 6-7). Follow method opposite. The quantities below are for a 20 × 30cm (8 × 12 in) Swiss roll tin (jelly roll pan).

★

90g (3 oz/⅓ cup) caster (superfine) sugar
3 eggs
90g (3 oz/¾ cup) plain (all-purpose) flour
½ tsp baking powder
flavourings, see below

★

FLAVOURINGS
Chocolate Substitute 15g (½ oz/2 tbsp) flour with cocoa (unsweetened cocoa powder).
Coffee Add 1 tbsp instant coffee with flour.

2 Invert cooked sponge onto sugared paper and peel off top paper. Trim cake edges. Make a shallow cut along one short side of the cake. If using a filling such as jam, warm gently and spread over warm cake. Alternatively, place second sheet of paper on top of sponge.

1 Preheat oven to 220°C (425°F/Gas 7). Prepare mixture as opposite; sifting baking powder with flour. Omit butter. Bake for 7-8 minutes, until firm when gently pressed. Spread out a clean, damp tea-towel. Top with greaseproof paper (parchment) dusted with caster (superfine) sugar.

3 Fold sponge on cut line and roll up, with filling or paper inside. Use sugared paper as a guide. Hold rolled sponge in position for a few seconds with join underneath. Peel cake off sugared paper; cool on wire rack. When cold, unroll, remove paper and spread with prepared filling. Re-roll cake.

American Sponge

This is a good base for novelty cakes or petits fours (see page 36). In advance, preheat oven, prepare tin (pan), pages 6-7. The quantities below are for a 20cm (8 in) round or 18cm (7 in) square cake. Double all quantities for a 23cm (9 in) round or a 20cm (8 in) square cake.

★

125g (4 oz) butter
185g (6 oz/³/₄ cup) caster (superfine) sugar
¹/₂ tsp vanilla essence (extract)
220g (7 oz/1³/₄ cups) plain (all-purpose)
flour
2 tsp baking powder
125ml (4 fl oz/¹/₂ cup) water
4 egg whites

★

2 Sift flour and baking powder together. Add to creamed mixture alternately with water, beating well between each addition, until smooth. In a clean, dry, grease-free bowl, whisk egg whites until stiff but not dry.

1 Preheat oven to 180°C (350°F/Gas 4). Beat butter, caster (superfine) sugar and vanilla together in a bowl until light and fluffy, using either a wooden spoon or an electric mixer.

3 Fold egg whites into cake mixture a little at a time, with a metal spoon. Use a figure-of-eight action to blend mixture; do not overmix. Scrape mixture into cake tin (pan). Bake 4-egg white mixture for 35-45 minutes; 8-egg white mixture for 55-65 minutes. Remove from tin, following Step 6, page 11.

Madeira Cake

Firm textured and easy to slice Madeira cake is perfect for cutting into shapes for novelty cakes.

★

250g (8 oz) butter, softened
250g (8 oz/1 cup) caster (superfine) sugar
grated rind and juice of 1 lemon or orange
5 eggs, beaten
220g (7 oz/1¾ cups) self-raising flour
90g (3 oz/¾ cup) plain (all-purpose) flour

★

● Preheat oven to 160°C (325°F/Gas 3). Fully line and grease a 20cm (8 in) round cake tin (pan) or an 18cm (7 in) square cake tin (see pages 6-7).
● In a warm bowl, cream butter and sugar with citrus rind, using either a wooden spoon or an electric mixer, until pale and fluffy.
● Gradually add eggs, beating well after each addition. A tablespoon of the flour, added with the eggs, will prevent curdling. Stir in juice.
● Sift flours together and gradually fold in, using a large metal tablespoon. Scrape mixture into tin (pan). Smooth surface. Bake for 1½ hours until firm to the touch. A skewer inserted in the centre of the cake should come out clean. Cool slightly in the tin, then invert on a wire rack to cool completely. Remove lining paper.

FLAVOURING

Chocolate Chip Add 60g (2 oz/⅓ cup) chocolate chips (bits) with citrus juice.
Double Chocolate Omit citrus rind and juice and substitute 30g (1 oz/¼ cup) plain (all-purpose) flour with 30g (1 oz/¼ cup) cocoa (unsweetened cocoa powder). Add 60g (2 oz/⅓ cup) chocolate chips (bits).

Chocolate Roulade

★

5 eggs, separated
185g (6 oz/¾ cup) caster (superfine) sugar
185g (6 oz/6 squares) white or plain (semisweet) chocolate
caster (superfine) sugar for dusting

★

● Preheat oven to 180°C (350°F/Gas 4). Line and grease 33 × 23cm (13 × 9 in) Swiss roll tin (jelly roll pan) (see page 6). Beat egg yolks with 155g (5 oz/⅔ cup) of the sugar until pale and thick. Melt chocolate, then stir it in. Add egg whites with remaining sugar, following instructions below. Transfer mixture to tin. Bake for 20 minutes. Cover with a dampened tea towel: cool. Invert onto greaseproof paper (parchment) dusted with caster sugar.

Whisk egg whites in a clean, greasefree bowl until stiff. Gradually beat in remaining caster (superfine) sugar. Using a large metal tablespoon, carefully fold into white or dark chocolate mixture. Do not beat or mixture will deflate and cake will not rise.

Chocolate Mousse Cake

As the name suggests, Chocolate Mousse Cake is very moist, rich and mousse-like in texture. Use either plain (semisweet) chocolate, milk (German sweet) or white chocolate – all types will give good although slightly different results. After the cake has been removed from the oven it will sink slightly in the tin (pan). This is perfectly normal and will not affect the flavour or texture. Once made, the cake can be decorated quite simply by being spread with a generous layer of soured or whipped cream and finished with chocolate curls or caraque (see page 30). For a more elaborate finish, try the Christmas wreath on page 86.

185g (6 oz/6 squares) plain (semisweet) chocolate
60g (2 oz) butter
6 eggs, separated
90g (3 oz/¹⁄₃ cup) caster (superfine) sugar
125g (4 oz/1 cup) ground almonds

● Preheat oven to 180°C (350°F/Gas 4). Base line and grease a 20cm (8 in) round cake tin (pan) (see page 7). Melt the chocolate with the butter in a bowl set over hot water.
● Using an electric mixer, whisk the egg yolks in a bowl with half the sugar until the mixture becomes thick and pale. Gradually whisk in the melted chocolate mixture.
● Thoroughly clean and dry the whisks, then beat the egg whites in a clean greasefree bowl until stiff peaks form. Add the remaining sugar gradually, whisking well after each addition so that mixture becomes thick and glossy. Fold in the ground almonds, following detailed instructions right.
● Using a large metal tablespoon, carefully fold the chocolate mixture into the whites until just incorporated.
● Scrape the mixture into the tin (pan) and bake for 40 minutes until the cake has a firm crust. Leave to cool in the tin. Loosen edges of cake with a knife before inverting onto a wire rack or plate. Remove lining paper.

EXPERT ADVICE

Chocolate Mousse Cake should be baked as soon as it is made as the mixture quickly loses bulk if kept standing. Once cooled, store in an airtight container for up to 2 days to prevent the cake from drying out.

As soon as egg whites are stiff gradually whisk in remaining sugar. Sprinkle ground almonds over egg whites and carefully fold in, using a large metal tablespoon, until only just combined.

Moist Rich Chocolate Cake

For ingredients, pan sizes and timings, see chart.

● Preheat oven to 160°C (325°F/Gas 3). Line and grease a cake tin (pan) (see page 6). Put the milk in a jug and add the vinegar. Set aside.

● Melt chocolate in a bowl set over a pan of hot water without bowl touching water. Combine margarine, sugar and eggs in a bowl. Sift together flour, bicarbonate of soda (baking soda) and the cocoa (unsweetened cocoa powder). Add to the bowl of margarine mixture with half the milk.

● Using either a wooden spoon or electric mixer, beat the mixture until smooth. Add melted chocolate and remaining milk and beat until combined.

● Scrape mixture into prepared tin (pan). Bake at once (see Expert Advice, page 66) for time stated in chart. A skewer inserted in the centre should come out clean. Cool in tin for 30 minutes, then transfer to a wire rack. Remove lining paper.

MOIST RICH CHOCOLATE CAKE – QUANTITIES CHART

Ingredients	Tin (Pan) Size		
	15cm (6 in) round or 13cm (5 in) square	20cm (8 in) round or 18cm (7 in) square	25cm (10 in) round or 23cm (9 in) square
milk	125ml (4 fl oz/½ cup)	250ml (8 fl oz/1 cup)	470ml (15 fl oz/1¾ cups)
vinegar	1 tsp	1 tbsp	2 tbsp
chocolate, plain (semisweet)	60g (2 oz/2 squares)	125g (4 oz/4 squares)	250g (8 oz/8 squares)
margarine, soft	60g (2 oz)	125g (4 oz)	250g (8 oz)
sugar, caster (superfine)	125g (4 oz/½ cup)	250g (8 oz/1 cup)	500g (1 lb/2 cups)
eggs	1	2	4
flour, self-raising	155g (5 oz/1¼ cups)	315g (10 oz/2½ cups)	685g (1 lb 6oz/5½ cups)
bicarbonate of soda (baking soda)	½ tsp	1 tsp	2 tsp
cocoa (unsweetened cocoa powder)	1 tbsp	2 tbsp	4 tbsp
Baking Time	**1 hour**	**1½ hours**	**2¼ hours**

Chocolate Fudge Cake

Flavoured with cocoa (unsweetened cocoa powder), Chocolate Fudge Cake has a very rich, dense texture. Top it with Chocolate Fudge Icing on page 24 or Ganache, see page 26. The cake is particularly thick, so use a deep sturdy tin (pan). If you prefer a shallower cake, use a 23 or 25cm (9 or 10 in) tin (pan).

★

250g (8 oz) butter, softened, or soft margarine
375g (12 oz/2 cups) soft dark brown sugar
375g (12 oz/3 cups) plain (all-purpose) flour
1 tbsp baking powder
4 eggs, lightly beaten
4 tbsp golden syrup (light corn syrup)
125g (4 oz/1 cup) cocoa (unsweetened cocoa powder)
185 ml (6 fl oz/³⁄₄ cup) warm water
155ml (¼ pt/²⁄₃ cup) plain yogurt

★

● Preheat oven to 150°C (300°F/Gas 2). Grease and fully line a 20cm (8 in) round cake tin (pan) or 18cm (7 in) square tin (pan) (see page 6).
● Combine butter or margarine and sugar in a large bowl and beat, using a wooden spoon or electric mixer, until pale and fluffy. Sift flour and baking powder together in a separate bowl.
● Gradually add beaten eggs to creamed mixture, beating well after each addition. A tablespoon of flour added to the mixture will prevent curdling.
● Stir in syrup. In a small bowl, blend cocoa (unsweetened cocoa powder) with measured water to make a paste. Beat into mixture in large bowl.
● Add flour mixture and yogurt, following detailed instructions below. Scrape into prepared tin (pan) and level surface with the back of the spoon. Bake for 1¼-1½ hours or until well risen. A skewer inserted in the centre of the cake should come out clean. Cool briefly in tin, then invert on a wire rack and leave to cool completely. Remove lining paper.

★ ★ ★ ★ ★ ★ ★

EXPERT ADVICE

Soured cream or crème fraîche may be used instead of the yogurt, and treacle (molasses or dark corn syrup) substituted for the golden syrup (light corn syrup) for an even darker and richer cake.

★ ★ ★ ★ ★ ★ ★

Using a large metal tablespoon, fold in half the sifted flour and baking powder mixture, using a figure-of-eight action. Fold in yogurt, then add remaining flour in the same way as before, until only just combined.

TOPPINGS & FILLINGS

Marzipan

Marzipan (almond paste) has several uses in cake decorating. It can be used to cover cakes before adding a layer of icing, or used as an alternative to icing as on the Battenburg Cake illustrated on page 52. Pliable in texture, it can also be moulded into novelty shapes. The chocolate ribbon on page 64 and roses on page 32 can be made in marzipan. The results will be slightly less delicate, but perfectly acceptable.

★

250g (8 oz/2 cups) ground almonds
125g (4 oz/½ cup) caster (superfine) sugar
125g (4 oz/¾ cup) icing
(confectioners') sugar
1 egg white
1 tsp lemon juice

★

● Place almonds and both sugars in a large bowl. Stir the ingredients together. Add egg white and lemon juice and mix until mixture starts to bind together. As soon as the mixture starts to form a paste, turn it out on a surface dusted with icing (confectioners') sugar. Knead paste lightly until completely smooth. Avoid over kneading which would make the paste soft and oily.
● When ready, wrap marzipan in foil or a polythene bag. Store in a cool place, or refrigerate for up to 3 days before using. Makes about 500g (1 lb).

FLAVOURING

Chocolate Marzipan (Almond Paste) Make as above, adding 45g (1½ oz/⅓ cup) sifted cocoa (unsweetened cocoa powder) to the sugar, and using 1 extra egg white.
Chocolate Hazelnut Paste Make as for Chocolate Marzipan above, substituting grounds hazelnuts for almonds.

Apricot Glaze

This is frequently brushed over cakes before they are coated with marzipan (almond paste) or pouring fondant. If using clear apricot jam it is not necessary to pass through a sieve.

★

250g (8 oz/1cup) apricot jam
2 tbsp lemon juice

★

● Warm jam in a small saucepan until melted. Press through a sieve into a clean pan and stir in lemon juice.
● Boil for approximately 30 seconds, then remove from heat. Allow to cool slightly, then apply to cake with a clean brush. Makes about 125ml (4 fl oz/½ cup).

Chocolate Moulding Icing

This is a variation of ordinary moulding icing or sugarpaste and is equally as versatile, whether used to cover a smart, special occasion cake or a novelty one. It can be made using plain (semisweet), dark dessert (German dark), milk (German sweet) or white chocolate. It can also be moulded into figures and decorations for cakes.

185g (6 oz/6 squares) plain (semisweet) chocolate
2 tbsp liquid glucose
1 egg white
500g (1 lb/3 cups) icing (confectioners') sugar, sifted

● Break up chocolate and place it in a small heatproof bowl over a saucepan of hot water so that the bowl is not actually touching the hot water.

● Add the liquid glucose and leave until melted. Remove from the heat and leave for 2 minutes, then add the egg white and a little of the icing (confectioners') sugar. Beat with an electric mixer until smooth, following detailed instructions right. Finally, wrap the paste in cling film (plastic wrap) or a polythene bag and keep in a cool place for up to 3 days. This amount is sufficient to cover a 20-23cm (8-9in) cake.

Beat chocolate mixture until smooth, gradually adding remaining icing (confectioners') sugar. When mixture becomes too stiff to beat, turn it onto a surface and knead in remaining icing sugar to make a stiff paste.

EXPERT ADVICE

For successful rolling and moulding, Chocolate Moulding Icing must be the correct consistency. If when rolled it becomes soft and sticks to the work surface, gather it up and knead in more icing (confectioners') sugar. If it is dry and cracks, heat it in the microwave on High for 30 seconds. If still dry, sprinkle with water and knead to soften.

Unlike ordinary sugarpaste, Chocolate Moulding Icing does not develop a dry crust if exposed to the air for more than a minute or two. It does, however, harden slowly as the chocolate sets. If this happens, heat it in the microwave on High for 30 seconds. Allow to stand for 1 minute, then microwave for a further 30 seconds if necessary. When rolling or moulding the icing, dust surface and hands with cornflour (cornstarch) to prevent sticking.

Basic Buttercream

This is sufficient to fill a 20-23cm (8-9 in) layer
cake. Double quantities to cover top and sides.

★

90g (3 oz) butter, softened
1 tbsp milk or hot water
185g (6 oz/1¼ cups) icing (confectioners')
sugar
food colouring, optional

★

FLAVOURINGS
Chocolate Buttercream Add 2 tbsp sifted
cocoa (unsweetened cocoa powder) with the
icing (confectioners') sugar.
Citrus Buttercream Add finely grated rind of
1 orange or lemon to the butter.

2 Sift in icing (confectioners') sugar with any
dry flavouring such as cocoa (unsweetened
cocoa powder). Gradually stir in sugar, then
beat hard until pale, light and fluffy. A little
extra liquid may be needed if a soft icing is
required.

1 Place butter in a large bowl. Gradually add
milk or water working mixture together
until creamy. For a less rich icing, a soft butter
and vegetable spread may be used, in which
case less liquid will be required. Grated citrus
rind may be added at this tage.

3 A little food colouring may be added during
the final beating. Pale colours may be
altered slightly by the butter content of the
icing; if colour is crucial, substitute white
vegetable fat (shortening).

Crème au Beurre

The basis of this rich icing is a sugar syrup which is added to beaten egg yolks before being combined with butter. Follow the step-by-step method shown here. The quantity below will cover a 20-cm (8-in) cake.

★

90g (3 oz/⅓ cup) caster (superfine) sugar
4 tbsp water
2 egg yolks
185g (6 oz) unsalted butter, softened
1 tsp vanilla or almond essence (extract),
optional

★

2 Beat softened butter in a separate bowl until light and fluffy. Gradually beat in syrup and egg mixture.

1 Gently heat the sugar and water in a pan until the sugar melts and the mixture becomes syrupy. Whisk egg yolks in a bowl until pale in colour. Pour in syrup slowly. Whisk until all the syrup has been incorporated and the mixture is thick.

3 Fold or beat in flavourings, if used. Above shows lemon juice and honey being added to the crème au beurre, as for Honey & Lemon Ring, see page 40.

Buttercream Paste

This versatile icing can be rolled out like marzipan and used to cover the top of a cake, making a dry, flat surface for piping and decorating. It may be made in advance and briefly stored but should not be refrigerated. Follow the step-by-step method shown here. Makes about 750g (1½ lb).

★

60g (2 oz) butter or white vegetable fat
(shortening)
2 tbsp lemon juice
2 tbsp water
625-750g (1¼-1½ lb/3¼-4½ cups) icing
(confectioners') sugar
food colouring and flavouring, optional

2 Stir in a further 185g (6 oz/1¼ cups) icing (confectioners') sugar. Remove from heat and pour into a bowl. Cool slightly, then beat in enough of the remaining sugar to make a pliable paste. Beat in colouring and/or flavouring, if used.

1 Melt fat with lemon juice and water in a saucepan over low heat. Stir in 185g (6 oz/ 1¼ cups) of the icing (confectioners') sugar. Continue to heat, stirring occasionally, for 2-3 minutes. Do not boil.

3 Knead paste in the bowl for a few moments, then transfer to a clean surface which has been lightly dusted with icing (confectioners') sugar. Knead paste until smooth and elastic. If not using at once, wrap thoroughly.

Chocolate Fudge Icing

This delicious icing turns a Victoria Sandwich Cake into a special treat. Have the cake filled and glazed before making the icing, which sets quickly. Follow step-by-step method shown here. Sufficient to cover a 20-23cm (8-9 in) cake.

★

250g (8 oz/8 squares) plain chocolate
(semisweet), broken up
125g (4 oz) butter
2 eggs
250g (8 oz/1½ cups) icing (confectioners')
sugar

★

2 Cool chocolate mixture slightly, then beat in eggs one at a time. Beat vigorously for about 30 seconds, then stir in icing (confectioners') sugar. Beat mixture until it begins to thicken and become pale. When ready, it should coat the back of the spoon.

1 Combine chocolate and butter in a large heatproof bowl. Set bowl over a saucepan of hot water and leave until chocolate and butter have melted.

3 Pour icing quickly over glazed cake, smoothing it with a warmed knife. Alternatively, continue beating until the icing forms soft peaks and is quite pale. Swirl it quickly and evenly over glazed cake with a small palette knife to create soft peaks.

Sugar Syrup

This syrup may be stored in a clean screw-topped jar for several weeks, but will crystallize if refrigerated.

250g (8 oz) granulated sugar
pinch of cream of tartar
4 tbsp water

Place sugar and cream of tartar in a heavy-bottomed saucepan. Add water and stir over moderate heat until sugar has melted. Continue to heat, without stirring, until syrup begins to bubble gently.

Boil without stirring until syrup measures 105°C/220°F on a sugar (candy) thermometer. Alternatively, test by dipping a teaspoon in the syrup and then pressing another teaspoon onto the back of it. Gently separate the spoons. If a fine thread forms, the syrup is ready.
Remove pan from heat immediately and plunge the bottom of it into ice cold water. This will prevent the syrup from caramelizing. When cool, pour into a clean warm glass jar with a screw top. If syrup thickens on standing, warm it gently by standing jar in warm water.

Glacé Icing

Glacé icing resembles a glaze. It cannot be piped, but makes an easy topping for simple chocolate cakes. It can be swirled with melted chocolate for a marbled effect, as the Milky Marble Cake illustrated on page 57, or flavoured with melted chocolate.

185g (6 oz/1¼ cups) icing (confectioners')
sugar
2-3 tsp warm water

Sift icing (confectioners') sugar into a small bowl. Gradually beat in water until icing thickly coats the back of the spoon. Use immediately or cover surface to prevent the formation of a crust. Sufficient to top a 20-23cm (8-9 in) cake.

VARIATIONS
Chocolate Glacé Icing Melt 60g (2 oz/ 2 squares) plain (semisweet) chocolate and stir in 15g (½ oz) butter. Add to the glacé icing.
Coffee Glacé Icing Mix the warm water with 1 tbsp instant coffee powder before adding to the icing (confectioners') sugar.

Ganache

There are several recipes for Chocolate Ganache, but all result in a deliciously smooth and creamy mixture which makes an irresistible filling or covering for cakes. Freshly made ganache has a pouring consistency. It thickens as it cools. For a smooth cake covering, use when the ganache thickly coats the back of the spoon. If left until completely cold and whisked, it becomes thick enough to use as a cake filling. It may also be piped into chocolate cases such as those illustrated on page 33, to make delicious petits fours. Plain (semisweet) or dark dessert (German dark) chocolate gives a rich, dark ganache, but milk (German sweet) or white chocolate may be substituted.

★

250g (8 oz/8 squares) plain (semisweet)
chocolate
155ml (¼ pt/⅔ cup) double (heavy)
cream

★

Melt chocolate in a heatproof bowl set over a pan of hot water. Place cream in a small heavy-bottomed saucepan and bring just to the boil. Complete following detailed instructions above right. Sufficient to cover top and sides of a 20-23cm (8-9 in) cake.

★ ★ ★ ★ ★ ★ ★

EXPERT ADVICE

For filling cakes and piping, cold ganache can be whisked with an electric mixer until paler in colour and increased in volume.

★ ★ ★ ★ ★ ★ ★

Slowly pour hot cream over chocolate, beating well with a balloon whisk until cream is incorporated and mixture is completely smooth. Chill, stirring occasionally; until ganache has reached the required consistency.

Crème Diplomate

★

3 tsp custard powder or 4 tsp cornflour
(cornstarch)
1 tbsp caster (superfine) sugar
155ml (¼ pt/⅔ cup) milk
155 ml (¼ pt/⅔ cup) double (heavy)
cream
few drops of vanilla essence (extract)

★

Blend custard powder or cornflour (cornstarch) and sugar with a little milk in a saucepan. Stir in remaining milk and cook over moderate heat, stirring constantly, until thick and smooth. Pour into a bowl, cover and chill. Whip cream until thick and fold into chilled custard with vanilla.

American Frosting

This meringue icing is firm on the outside and soft underneath. It can be used as a delicious filling or covering for cakes. Follow the step-by-step method shown here. Sufficient to cover a 20cm (8 in) cake.

★

250g (8 oz/1 cup) granulated
sugar
pinch of cream of tartar
4 tbsp water
2 egg whites

★

2 Whisk egg whites in a clean, greasefree bowl until very stiff. Holding the pan of syrup high above the bowl, pour it in carefully in a steady stream, constantly whisking the mixture until all the syrup has been incorporated.

1 Using the sugar, cream of tartar and measured water, make a syrup as above, continuing to heat the mixture until it registers 115°C/240°F on a sugar (candy) thermometer. Alternatively, test by dropping ½ tsp syrup into a bowl of cold water. If you can mould it to a soft ball the syrup is ready.

3 Whisk in any flavouring or colouring, then continue to whisk mixture until soft peaks form when the whisk is lifted. Quickly spread frosting over prepared cake, drawing it into peaks or swirls with a warm dry palette knife.

Chocolate Frosting

⭐

*60g (2 oz/2 squares) plain (semisweet)
chocolate
185g (6 oz/¾ cup) caster (superfine) sugar
1 egg white
pinch of cream of tartar*

⭐

Melt the chocolate in a heatproof bowl over hot water. Combine the sugar, egg white and cream of tartar in a large heatproof bowl. Place the bowl over a saucepan of gently simmering water. Using an electric mixer beat ingredients together until mixture forms soft peaks. This will take 6-8 minutes. Continue, following instructions below. Sufficient to cover an 18-20 cm (7-8 in) cake.

Remove bowl from heat. Gradually whisk melted chocolate into egg white until evenly incorporated. Immediately spread frosting over top and sides of cake, using a palette knife to spread and swirl mixture.

Fondant

There is a great deal of confusion about fondant, largely because the term was at one time applied to sugarpaste and other moulding icings. Fondant is a pouring icing, traditionally used on petits fours, which has at its base a white paste that should be made in advance and diluted with syrup when required. Step-by-step instructions for making the basic fondant mixture are given opposite, while the recipe for Petits Fours on page 36 illustrates its use.

⭐

*500g (1 lb/2 cups) caster (superfine) sugar
3 tsp liquid glucose or pinch of cream of
tartar
6 tbsp water*

⭐

1 Gently heat the sugar, glucose or cream of tartar and water until the sugar melts and the mixture becomes syrupy. Pour it onto a wetted marble slab or cool greasefree surface and cool slightly.

2 Using two scrapers or spatulas, scrape the syrup from the sides to the centre, using a figure-of-eight movement. Continue working the fondant in this fashion for about 5 minutes or until it forms a stiff white paste.

3 Break off pieces of fondant and knead until smooth. Finally knead pieces together to form a ball. Place in a bowl, cover with a damp clean cloth and leave for 24 hours before storing in a screw-topped jar. Do not store in the refrigerator.

4 To prepare a pouring fondant icing, place fondant in a clean bowl over a saucepan of hot (not boiling) water. Stir occasionally until melted. Add 1 tbsp sugar syrup. Continue to heat, adding more syrup if necessary, until it coats the back of the spoon.

EXPERT ADVICE

Make fondant at least 24 hours before it is required, so that paste can mature. When preparing fondant it is important to keep the sides of the pan free of sugar crystals. A dampened pastry brush is ideal for this purpose. Allow plenty of time for working and kneading paste. Store in a tightly covered jar in a cool place (not the refrigerator) for up to two months. Before fondant can be used, it must be melted over gentle heat. Avoid overheating, which could spoil the glossy appearance. Sugar syrup is frequently added to create the correct consistency for pouring. At this stage a very few drops of colouring or flavouring may be added.

CHOCOLATE DECORATIONS

Chocolate Caraque & Curls

Given a little time, professional looking scrolls or chocolate caraque can be made. For every-day cakes, press pared curls or grated chocolate around the sides, as for the Milky Marble Cake page 57. Caraque and curls quickly soften, so should be kept in a very cool place.

CARAQUE

Melt 250g (8 oz/8 squares) plain (semisweet) chocolate and pour onto a marble slab or other clean smooth surface. Leave until set.
Use a long knife with a rigid blade. Hold knife at angle of 45° to the chocolate. Draw it lightly across to cut thin layers that curl into scrolls. Fans are made in the same way, using the end of a round-bladed knife.

CURLS

Using a potato peeler, pare away curls from a bar or slab of plain (semisweet) chocolate, milk (German sweet) or white chocolate. If the chocolate is too cold it may be brittle. Leave in a warm place for a few minutes, or heat briefly in the microwave before trying again.

GRATED CHOCOLATE

Grated chocolate is useful for melting into sauces or as a speedy alternative to curls for decorating the sides of a cake. Use the coarse blades of a metal grater.

✱ ✱ ✱ ✱ ✱ ✱ ✱

EXPERT ADVICE

If the chocolate fails to form scrolls, try adjusting the angle of the knife. If too cold, the chocolate may break off in brittle pieces. Leave in a warm place for a few minutes and try again.

✱ ✱ ✱ ✱ ✱ ✱ ✱

Chocolate Cutouts & Boxes

Melted chocolate can be thinly spread on greaseproof paper (parchment) and left to set, ready for cutting out numerous novelty shapes or dainty boxes. A simple cake for a child's birthday could be made by cutting out milk (semisweet) chocolate shapes and securing them to a cake covered in white chocolate. Squares or panels of chocolate can also be made for covering the tops or sides of cakes, a technique which has been used to good effect on the Chequered Chocolate Parcel illustrated on page 65 and the White Chocolate Box illustrated on page 61.

CHOCOLATE CUTOUTS

Melt plain (semisweet), milk (German sweet) or white chocolate in a bowl over hot water. Pour onto a sheet of greaseproof paper (parchment) or wax paper.

Spread chocolate with a knife to thinly cover the paper. Gently lift up the paper at the edges and shake lightly so that the chocolate forms a smooth layer.

Leave in a cool place until set. Using metal biscuit (cookie) cutters, cut out shapes and lift away from the paper.

CHOCOLATE BOXES

These can be made in miniature *petit four* sizes or slightly larger for individual cakes. For each box cut out five equal squares of chocolate, each 2.5cm (1 in) in diameter. Place one square on surface and cover with 1cm (½ in) square of chocolate sponge. Spread a little whipped cream or Ganache (see page 26) over the sponge, then secure the four remaining squares around the cream to make a box. Finish with strawberries or other fresh fruit and sprigs of mint or chocolate leaves. For larger chocolate boxes increase the size of squares to 4cm (1½ in) and use 2.5cm (1 in) squares of sponge.

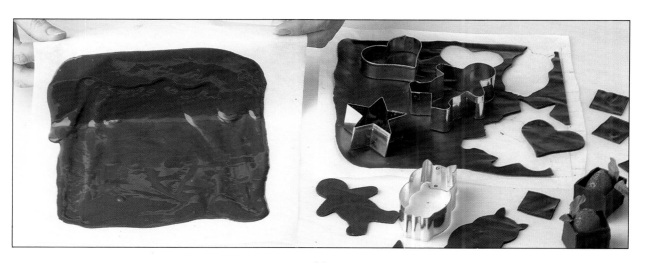

Modelling Chocolate

Modelling chocolate is made from a mixture of chocolate and liquid glucose. It is very easy to manage and it can be shaped into various different stunning flowers, figures, ribbons, bows and novelty shapes. Instructions are given here for modelling roses, but with a little practice the possibilities are endless, particularly if you use a mixture of plain (semisweet), milk (German sweet) and white chocolate as this is easier to work with. To make 155g (5 oz) modelling chocolate you will need 125g (4 oz/4 squares) chocolate and 2 tbsp liquid glucose.

Melt the chocolate in a heatproof bowl over hot but not boiling water. Remove from the heat and beat in the glucose until a paste is formed. Continue beating until the mixture comes away from the sides of the bowl. Place the paste in a polythene bag and chill for about 1 hour until firm but pliable. (See also Expert Advice, page 63). If chocolate becomes too firm allow to stand in a warm place for 5 minutes.

Chocolate Roses

To make a chocolate rose, take a piece of modelling chocolate about the size of a grape; shape into a cone. Keep the remaining modelling chocolate covered in the polythene bag so it does not dry out. Press down on the surface of the cone and squeeze a 'waist' into the cone near the base. Take another piece of paste about half the size of the cone and press it as flat as possible between your fingers to create a petal shape. Secure this around the cone. Shape another slightly larger petal and wrap this around the first, overlapping it slightly. Continue building up the petals to form the rose, making each petal slightly larger than the previous one, until you have a complete rose of 7-8 petals, as illustrated below. Bend and tuck the other petals to create a realistic shape. Once completed, slice just below the petals; use the base to shape the next cone. To create a posy, vary the sizes of the roses. For buds use just 3-4 petals, tucking them tightly around the cone.

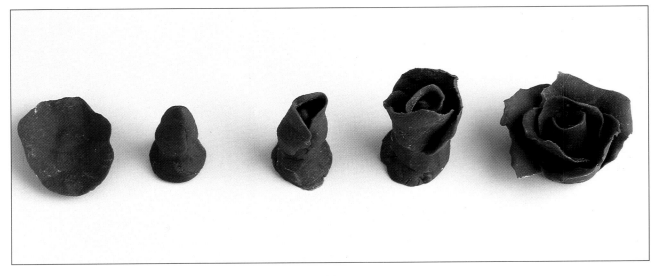

Chocolate Leaves

These make some of the easiest yet most effective decorations for any type of chocolate cake, whether as a covering for the whole cake, as in the Christmas Wreath illustrated on page 87, or simply to complete an arrangement of chocolate roses. Virtually any non-poisonous leaf may be used as a mould as long as they are not blemished and are not too delicate. Rose, lemon balm, mint, bay leaves and holly all work extremely well. To cover about 20 leaves you will need 90g (3 oz/3 squares) plain (semisweet), milk (German sweet), dark dessert (German dark) chocolate or milk chocolate. Try swirling dark and light chocolate together in the bowl very lightly and then brush over the leaves to form a marbled effect. Instructions for coating are given below.

Gently wipe leaves with a damp cloth. Using a clean paintbrush, thickly coat underside of each leaf with melted chocolate. Lay flat on wax paper, chocolate side up, until set, then carefully peel leaves off chocolate.

Chocolate Cases

Small *petit four* or paper sweet cases (candy cups) make perfect moulds for shaping chocolate cases. These can be filled with piped Ganache (see page 26), used as a container for whipped cream or lemon mousse or scattered over a chocolate cake for decoration, as on the White Chocolate Box illustrated on page 61. They also make tasty containers for truffles. To coat about 20 paper sweet cases you will need 125g (4 oz/4 squares) plain (semisweet), milk (German sweet) or white chocolate, melted. For delightful Christmas or special homemade gifts coat some gold and silver sweet cases with chocolate. Fill with desired flavour of filling and package in small decorative bags, tied with ribbons. Instructions for coating paper cases (candy cups) are given below.

Using the back of a small teaspoon thickly coat base and sides of paper cases (candy cups). Scoop out excess chocolate, then invert cases to set. When set check sides for any thinly coated areas; re-coat if necessary. Peel away paper.

TEA-TIME FAVOURITES

★

Tea time is the traditional time of day for cakes and this chapter includes recipes for many all-time favourites. Tempt your family and friends with the rich chocolate fudge cake or mocha gateau, or, if you prefer something lighter, try the honey and lemon sponge ring or the dainty petits fours. You will find a cake to suit everyone and all the recipes are easy to follow.

PETITS FOURS

These iced shapes may be filled with buttercream or with fresh cream.

★

4-egg white American Sponge mixture, see page 14.
FILLING AND COATING
1 quantity Basic Buttercream, see page 21
Apricot Glaze, see page 19
double quantity Fondant, see page 28
Sugar Syrup, see page 25
¼ tsp instant coffee dissolved in ½ tsp hot water
additional flavourings and colourings as desired
DECORATION
use any or all of the following: marzipan (almond paste), glacé (candied) cherries, blanched almonds, stem (preserved) ginger, crystallized rose petals or violets, chocolate motifs, see page 32

★

● Preheat the oven to 180°C (350°F/Gas 4). Line and grease a 20cm (8 in) square cake tin (pan). Prepare American Sponge cake as directed and bake for 35-45 minutes. Cool on a wire rack.
● Warm fondant, dissolving it in a clean bowl over a saucepan of hot water, add some sugar syrup to form the consistency of thick cream, see page 29. Flavour some of the fondant icing in a small bowl with the coffee and tint or flavour the rest as desired. Cut up, ice and decorate the cakes, following the step-by-step instructions right. When fondant has set, trim the base of each cake neatly with a sharp knife.

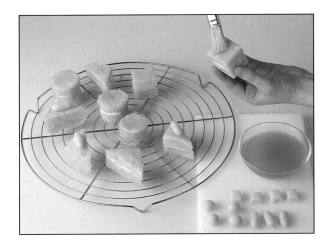

1 Cut cake in half horizontally, brushing off any crumbs. Spread cut halves with buttercream and sandwich back together. Cut into neat shapes, brushing away crumbs. Coat with apricot glaze. Place a marzipan roll, nut or half glacé (candied) cherry on top of each cake.

2 Place cakes well apart on a wire rack over wax paper. Pour fondant icing over each cake, letting it trickle down the sides. If free from crumbs, fondant that falls onto the paper may be used again. Decorate as desired.

RICH CHOCOLATE FUDGE CAKE

A traditional recipe, deliciously rich and tasty. The chocolate caraque gives a highly professional-looking finish.

⭐

20cm (8 in) round Chocolate Fudge Cake, see page 18
ICING AND DECORATION
155ml (¼ pt/⅔ cup) double (heavy) cream
2 tsp icing (confectioners') sugar, plus extra for dusting
1 quantity Chocolate Fudge Icing, see page 24
1 quantity chocolate caraque, see page 30

⭐

● Using a long serrated knife, split the cake in half horizontally. Place the bottom half on a flat serving place. Combine cream and icing (confectioners') sugar in a bowl and whisk to soft peaks. Sandwich cake together.

● Using a palette knife, spread about half the Chocolate Fudge Icing around sides of cake. Spoon remaining icing over top. Spread icing to cover cake evenly, then use tip of palette knife to mark a diagonal line from centre of top of cake down to base, as illustrated opposite. Repeat at 1cm (½ in) intervals all around cake to give a neat finish.

● Carefully arrange some of the chocolate caraque on top of the cake. Add remaining pieces, placing them at different angles to create an informal but symmetrical effect.

● Cut three strips of greaseproof paper (parchment), each about 2.5cm (1 in) wide. Lightly lay strips over caraque, then dust cake with icing (confectioners') sugar, following instructions right.

EXPERT ADVICE

To save time, coarsely grated chocolate (see page 30) can be used instead of caraque. To ensure that chocolate curls stick to icing, position them while icing is still soft. Removing greaseproof paper (parchment) strips from cake requires steady hands. Lift strips off one by one.
Try to avoid moving cake once it has been dusted with icing (confectioners') sugar. If you have to transport it, take paper and sugar with you and complete cake when you reach your destination.

Put a little icing (confectioners') sugar in fine sieve or tea strainer and use to heavily dust the top of the cake. Carefully lift off greaseproof paper (parchment) strips to reveal contrast between dusted and plain areas.

HONEY & LEMON RING

A rich honey and rum glaze soaks into this cake to provide a taste of the unexpected under the lemon-flavoured buttercream topping.

★

4-egg white American Sponge mixture, see page 14
TOPPING
2 lemons
4 tbsp clear honey
2 tbsp rum
1 quantity Crème au beurre, see page 22
LEMON STRANDS & LIME TWISTS
1 lemon, rind only
1 lime
2 tbsp caster (superfine) sugar

★

● Preheat oven to 180°C (350°F/Gas 4). Bake cake in a lined and greased 1.1 litre (2 pt/5 cup) ring tin (tube pan) for 25-30 minutes.
● Meanwhile make glazed lemon strands and lime twists, following the instructions right.
● Invert cake on a wire rack. Wash and dry the tin (pan) and place a ring of greaseproof paper (parchment) in the base. Return the warm cake to the tin.
● Make topping. Grate one of the lemons and squeeze them both. Set grated rind aside. Reserve 4 tsp of the lemon juice. Pour remaining juice into a small saucepan. Stir in half the honey and all the rum. Heat, without boiling, until honey melts, then pour mixture slowly over cake. Leave to cool in tin (pan). When quite cold, carefully transfer to a serving plate.
● Make crème au beurre. Beat in reserved lemon rind and juice with remaining honey, see step 3, page 22. Spread icing over cake,

smoothing it with a small palette knife. Holding the prongs of a fork against the side of the cake, slowly rotate the plate to create a design. Mark the top of the cake in a similar fashion, following illustration opposite. Decorate the top of the ring with the glazed lemon strands. Make a cut in each lime slice from outer edge to centre; twist slices. Add lime twists to the top of the cake. If not serving at once, store cake in a cool place. Eat within two days.

LEMON STRANDS AND LIME TWISTS
Cut thinly pared lemon rind into strands. Thinly slice lime. Place in a pan with water to cover; simmer for 5 minutes. Remove strands/slices with slotted spoon. Add sugar to pan; stir until dissolved. Boil, without stirring, until pale brown. Return strands/slices. When caramel coated, remove and spread out on a plate to dry. Twist slices, following instructions above.

BLACK FOREST CAKE

A perennial favourite, Black Forest Cake is a chocoholic's dream. This was originally a classic Austrian delicacy. It is sometimes made with a cherry brandy called Kirsch, which comes from the Black Forest. It is a dazzling party cake.

⭐

4-egg chocolate-flavoured Genoese
Sponge mixture, see page 12
1 quantity Ganache, see page 26
250g (8 oz/¾ cup) while fruit morello
cherry jam
2 tbsp lemon juice
2 tbsp maraschino syrup
DECORATION
3 maraschino cherries
125g (4 oz/4 squares) cooking chocolate
60g (2 oz/2 squares) white chocolate
3 small rose leaves

⭐

● Preheat oven to 180°C (350°F/Gas 4). Bake cake in two lined and greased 20cm (8 in) round cake tins (pans). Cool on a wire rack.
● Make up Ganache mixture. Refrigerate until completely cold before whisking. Meanwhile melt the cooking and white chocolates and make chocolate caraque following the instructions on page 30, and the leaves on page 33. Use dark chocolate for caraque and white chocolate for cherries and leaves. See Expert Advice, right for dipping cherries.
● Combine jam, lemon juice and maraschino syrup in saucepan. Stir over low heat until jam has softened. Brush melted jam liberally over both sponge layers to cover, then spoon out cherries from the jam that are remaining in saucepan and spread them over the top of one of the cakes to form the base cake.
● Whisk cold ganache until pale in colour and doubled in volume. Spread one third of it over the cherries on the base cake. Place second sponge cake on top, jam side down. Spread remaining ganache over top and side of the cake and smooth over the surface with a palette knife. Press chocolate scrolls neatly around side of cake and arrange half-dipped cherries and leaves on top. Chill cake before serving.

⭐ ⭐ ⭐ ⭐ ⭐ ⭐ ⭐ ⭐

EXPERT ADVICE

To dip the maraschino cherries, drain them from the syrup and dry very well with absorbent kitchen paper. If they are still moist on the surface the chocolate will not stick well. Half-dip them in melted, warm white chocolate, then leave to dry on wax paper.

⭐ ⭐ ⭐ ⭐ ⭐ ⭐ ⭐ ⭐

COFFEE & WALNUT CAKE

Delicious meringue frosting, crisp on the outside yet creamy underneath, gives this delectable coffee cake a touch of real class.

⭐

6-egg coffee-flavoured Genoese Sponge mixture, see page 12
10 walnuts to decorate
FILLING AND COATING
250ml (8 fl oz/1 cup) double (heavy) cream
125ml (4 fl oz/½ cup) strong black coffee, chilled
3 tbsp icing (confectioners') sugar
60g (2 oz/½ cup) finely chopped walnuts
double quantity American Frosting, see page 27

⭐

● Preheat oven to 180°C (350°F/Gas 4). Bake cake in three lined and greased 20cm (8 in) round cake tins (pans). Cool each layer on a wire rack.

● Make the cream filling, see instructions right. Using half the cream filling for each layer, spread cream over two sponges and sprinkle each with chopped walnuts. Layer one cream-covered sponge on top of the other and then place the plain sponge on top.

● Place a small circle of wax paper or foil on top of an upturned plate with a diameter slightly less than that of the cake. Place cake on top of paper. Put cake in a cool place.

● Make frosting and quickly spread it over top and side of cream-filled cake. As icing begins to set, swirl it with a warm dry palette knife to form peaks. When set, carefully slide cake onto

a serving plate. Decorate the cake with walnuts. If liked, walnuts may first be glazed. Follow the instructions for glazing lemon strands and lime slices on page 40. Keep gâteau in a cool place (not the refrigerator). This gateau is best served the same day.

CREAM FILLING

In a bowl, whip cream to soft peaks, then continue whipping while slowly adding coffee in a thin steady stream. Gradually add icing (confectioners') sugar, continuing to whip cream until thick.

RICH VELVET CROWN CAKE

*Rich Chocolate Fudge Icing coats the
simple Victoria Sandwich Cake mixture
turning the cake into a luscious
tea-time favourite.*

★

*3-egg Victoria Sandwich Cake mixture,
see page 10
90g (3 oz/3 squares) plain (semisweet)
chocolate, melted*
TOPPING AND DECORATION
*60g (2 oz/2 squares) cooking chocolate
125g (4 oz/4 squares) white chocolate
Apricot Glaze, warmed, see page 19
1 quantity Chocolate Fudge Icing, page 24
2 tsp icing (confectioners') sugar*

★

● Preheat oven to 190°C (375°F/Gas 5). Base
line and grease a 1.1 litre (2 pt/5 cup) ring tin
(tube pan). Make a paper piping bag, see
instructions right. Melt cooking chocolate and
half the white chocolate in separate bowls and
make chocolate fans, see page 30.
● Divide cake mixture between two bowls and
fold the melted chocolate into one of them. Put
spoonfuls of the mixtures into the tin (pan),
drawing a skewer through the mixture. Bake
for 20-25 minutes. Cool on a wire rack,
removing lining paper and brush all over with
apricot glaze.
● Pour the chocolate icing round the top of
the cake so it covers the sides. Smooth with a
palette knife. Transfer to a plate when set.
● Melt remaining white chocolate. Stir in icing
(confectioners') sugar until dissolved. Spoon
mixture into piping bag. Pipe lines up the sides
and over the top of the cake. Place alternate
dark and white chocolate fans around the top,
as shown opposite.

1 Cut a piece of greaseproof paper
(parchment) into a rectangle measuring 25
× 20 cm (10 × 8 in). Cut the paper in half
diagonally and place one piece flat on table with
small point nearest to you. Fold right-hand
point over to centre point, making a cone. Hold
in position.

2 Lift the paper. Pick up the final point with
the right hand and wrap it over the cone so
that all three points meet together underneath.
Fold the points over twice to secure the cone.
For plain icing, snip off the pointed end of the
cone or insert writing tube (tip).

ALMOND MERINGUE GATEAU

Meringue, praline and crème pâtissière turn a simple sponge into a special cake.

★

*3-egg Victoria Sandwich Cake mixture,
see page 10
1 egg white
60g (2 oz/¼ cup) caster (superfine) sugar
60g (2 oz/¼ cup) ground almonds
almond essence (extract) to taste*
FILLING AND COATING
*125ml (4 fl oz/½ cup) double (heavy)
cream
1 quantity chilled Crème au Beurre
see page 22
almond essence (extract) to taste*
PRALINE
*185g (6 oz/1½ cups) whole blanched
almonds
185g (6 oz/¾ cup) caster (superfine) sugar*

★

● Preheat oven to 190°C (375°F/Gas 5). Divide cake mixture between two lined and greased 20cm (8 in) round cake tins (pans).
● Whisk egg white in a clean, greasefree bowl until stiff, then fold in sugar, ground almonds and essence (extract). Spread meringue over cake mixture in one of the tins (pans). Bake plain cake layer for 20-25 minutes; meringue layer for about 5 minutes longer. Remove from tins and cool on a wire rack, with meringue topping uppermost.
● Make praline. Combine almonds and sugar in a small heavy-bottomed saucepan. Stir over low heat until sugar has dissolved and turned a pale caramel colour. Spoon out 20 caramelized almonds and set aside for topping. Tip remaining mixture onto an oiled baking sheet. Set

aside to cool, then place in a strong polythene bag and crush with a rolling pin. Tip crushed praline into a sieve set over a bowl. Reserve both sieved and crushed praline.
● In a bowl, whip cream until stiff. Fold into chilled crème pâtissière with the almond essence (extract). Spread one third of the almond-flavoured cream over meringue-topped cake layer. Place plain layer on top. Set aside one third of the remaining cream and use the rest to coat the sides of the cake.
● Chill cake and reserved cream for 30 minutes. Coat side of cake in crushed praline, following instructions below. Spread remaining cream over top of cake, taking care not to disturb praline coating on sides. Arrange reserved caramelized almonds around rim. Mark lines on topping and dust them with the reserved sieved praline as illustrated opposite.

COATING THE SIDE OF THE CAKE
Sprinkle praline (or other coating) thickly along a piece of greaseproof paper (parchment) or foil. Place one hand on top of the cake and the other underneath it. Turn the cake and roll it lightly over the praline. Do not press heavily or the sides will be unevenly coated.

WHITE CHOCOLATE ROULADE

This wonderfully moist rolled cake is perfect for tea time. Plain (semisweet) chocolate may be used in place of white chocolate.

✱

*1 Chocolate Roulade made with white chocolate, see page 15
caster (superfine) sugar for dusting
60g (2 oz/½ cup) hazelnuts
1 quantity Crème au Beurre flavoured with 60g (2 oz/2 squares) white chocolate, melted, see page 22
icing (confectioners') sugar for dusting
pink food colouring
pink roses, optional, to decorate*

✱

● Bake chocolate roulade and leave to cool in tin (pan). Invert onto a sheet of greaseproof paper (parchment) dusted with caster (superfine) sugar. Remove lining paper, then invert cake onto a second piece of greaseproof paper so crust faces upwards. Trim all edges.
● Roughly chop hazelnuts and brown under a moderate grill until lightly toasted, stirring occasionally so they do not burn. Leave to cool, then beat into crème au beurre. Fill and roll up roulade, following instructions right.
● Put a little icing (confectioners') sugar in a bowl. Add a few drops of food colour (or dots of paste) and work in, using the back of a teaspoon. Continue working in colour until sugar is pale pink.
● Dust a flat rectangular serving plate generously with some white icing (confectioners') sugar, then with pink sugar. Position roulade on plate and dust with more sugar. Decorate with pink roses, if desired.

EXPERT ADVICE

*For a dinner party dessert, prepare both roulade and crème au beurre the day before; assemble up to 4 hours before serving. Dust roulade with icing (confectioners') sugar just before serving.
Sugared rose petals make a pretty decoration and can be prepared well in advance. Brush petals with lightly beaten egg white, dust with caster (superfine) sugar and leave on a wire rack for several hours to dry.*

Using a large palette knife spread the crème au beurre over the roulade to within 1cm (½ in) of edges. Starting from a short side, and using the greaseproof paper (parchment) as a guide, carefully roll up roulade.

BATTENBURG

This very impressive looking cake is surprisingly simple to make although it requires some time to assemble the pieces. The miniature Battenburgs add something special to the whole presentation.

★

*3-egg Quick Mix Cake mixture,
see page 10
pink food colouring
1 tbsp cocoa (unsweetened cocoa powder)
1 tbsp boiling water*
ASSEMBLY AND DECORATION
*½ quantity Apricot Glaze, see page 19
1 quantity Chocolate Marzipan (almond
paste), see page 19
½ quantity plain Marzipan (almond
paste), see page 19
icing (confectioners') sugar for dusting
20cm (8 in) cake board*

★

● Preheat oven to 160°C (325°F/Gas 3). Using card, divide an 18cm (7 in) square cake tin (pan) into two equal halves, securing card at ends with tape. Line and grease each half.
● Divide cake mixture equally between two bowls and beat a few drops of pink food colouring into one of them. (Do not make mixture too pink as colour will deepen during cooking.) Mix cocoa and water together and beat into remaining bowl of mixture. Spoon chocolate mixture into one side of tin and level surface. Spoon pink-coloured mixture into other side and level. Bake for about 40 minutes until firm. Cool; remove lining paper.
● Level cakes by cutting off domed tops. Slice each cake in half lengthways. Brush top of one

pink cake with apricot glaze; top with chocolate cake. Repeat with remaining cakes, reversing colours, then stick cakes together.
● Knead a small piece of the chocolate marzipan (almond paste) into a quarter of the plain marzipan until it is the same colour as the chocolate cake. Colour remaining plain marzipan same shade of pink as cake.
● Roll out two thirds of the pink marzipan (almond paste) as thinly as possible on a surface dusted with icing (confectioners') sugar. Lightly dampen cake board. Lay pink marzipan over board and trim off excess.
● Mould cake-coloured and remaining pink marzipan (almond paste) into two blocks, each about 10 × 2.5 × 1cm (4 × 1 × ½ in). Cut up and assemble into miniature Battenburg as for the cake. Trim long sides of both marzipan and cake Battenburg to give neat edges. Brush long sides of cake with remaining glaze.
● Lightly knead three quarters of the remaining chocolate marzipan (almond paste). Roll out on a sheet of wax paper to a rectangle, about 26 × 20 cm (14 × 8 in). Place cake on chocolate marzipan and trim off excess marzipan at both ends of cake. Neaten on trimmed ends, making sure there is sufficient marzipan to cover sides and meet over top of cake.
● Using wax paper as a guide, bring marzipan up over cake to meet in the middle. Join ends, trim off any excess paste. Cut a thin slice from either end of cake to neaten. Use remaining chocolate marzipan to cover miniature Battenburg in the same way.
● Carefully transfer cake to covered board, making sure that join is underneath. Cut miniature Battenburg in 1cm (½ in) slices and scatter them over the top and on the board.

MOCHA GATEAU

This cake uses a Genoese cake base, but a Victoria Sandwich or Moist Rich Chocolate Cake could be used instead. The coffee flavouring added to both sponge and icing can be omitted if a plain chocolate gâteau is preferred.

★

4-egg coffee-flavoured Genoese Sponge mixture, see page 12
155ml (¼pt/⅔ cup) double (heavy) cream
1 tbsp icing (confectioners') sugar
¼ tsp vanilla essence (extract)
1 tbsp instant coffee powder
2 tsp boiling water
1 quantity Ganache, see page 26
DECORATION
60g (2 oz/2 squares) plain (semisweet) chocolate
1m (1 yd 3 in) cream ribbon, about 4cm (1½ in) wide
1m (1 yd 3 in) brown ribbon, about 1.5cm (¾ in) wide

★

● Preheat oven to 180°C (350°F/Gas 4). Bake cake in two base-lined and greased 20cm (8 in) round cake tins (pans). Cool on a wire rack. Remove lining paper.

● In a bowl, whip cream to soft peaks, then while whipping gradually add icing (confectioners') sugar and vanilla. Use to sandwich cakes together. Place on a flat serving plate.

● Dissolve coffee powder in measured boiling water in a cup. Make ganache mixture, adding the coffee after the cream. Leave until mixture is thickened but remains level in bowl.

● Pour ganache over cake starting from the centre and working out, smooth down sides using a palette knife. Leave in a cool place to set.

● To make the chocolate lace motifs, make several tracings of the template on page 92 on the same piece of paper. You will need about 35 motifs, allowing for a few breakages. Secure tracings to a flat surface with a smooth piece of wax paper on top. Melt chocolate, put it in a paper piping bag fitted with a writing tube (tip) and quickly pipe over lace motif outlines. Leave to set.

● Using an upturned bowl, cutter or pan, about 18cm (7 in) in diameter and with a very fine rim, carefully mark a central circle on top of cake. Decorate cake top with chocolate motifs, following instructions below. Chill until set.

● Just before serving, wrap ribbons around cake as illustrated opposite.

Carefully peel paper away from chocolate lace. Gently press motifs into the ganache around the marked circle, tilting each backwards and spacing them slightly apart.

MILKY MARBLE CAKE

A simple tea-time cake, this cake is cleverly marbled in both sponge and icing with chocolate and cocoa with the sides lavishly coated with chocolate curls.

Madeira Cake mixture, see page 15
2 tbsp cocoa (unsweetened cocoa powder)
1 tbsp boiling water
1 tsp vanilla essence (extract)
grated rind of 1 lemon
ICING AND DECORATION
220g (7 oz/7 squares) milk (German sweet) chocolate
125g (4 oz/³/₄ cup) icing (confectioners') sugar
1 tbsp lemon juice

Preheat oven to 160°C (325°F/Gas 3). Base line and grease a 20cm (8 in) round cake tin (pan).

Divide cake mixture between two bowls. Beat cocoa (unsweetened cocoa powder) and boiling water together and add to one bowl. Stir vanilla essence (extract) and lemon rind into remaining bowl.

Put alternate spoonfuls of chocolate and lemon-flavoured mixture into tin (pan), occasionally drawing a skewer through the mixture. Bake for about 1½ hours or until a skewer inserted into the centre of the cake comes out clean. Cool on a wire rack. Remove lining paper.

Using 90g (3 oz/3 squares) of the chocolate, make curls, following instructions on page 30. Spread curls out thickly on a sheet of grease-proof paper (parchment). Melt remaining chocolate in a bowl set over hot water, and set 2 tbsp aside. Spread rest of melted chocolate around sides of marble cake.

While chocolate is still soft, coat side of cake in chocolate curls. The easiest way to do this is to place one hand palm down on top of the cake and the other palm up underneath it. Turn cake and roll it lightly in the chocolate curls, see page 48. Do not press heavily or the sides will be unevenly coated.

Place cake on a serving plate. Sift icing (confectioners') sugar into a bowl. Add lemon juice and mix glacé icing together to form the consistency of pouring cream. Spoon glacé icing onto top of cake and marble the icing with the melted chocolate using a cocktail stick (toothpick) and following the instructions below.

Spread glacé icing to edges of cake. Drizzle reserved 2 tbsp melted chocolate over icing. While still soft, run the tip of a cocktail stick (toothpick) through chocolate and icing to create the marbled effect.

CELEBRATION CAKES

★

Birthdays, Christmas, Easter and
Valentine's Day are all occasions to
celebrate and how better than with a
glorious celebration cake? This
section features many delicious and
unusual cakes to make for those
special occasions, or more often if you
prefer. There are recipes for a
wonderful chocolate box cake, a
surprise birthday parcel cake, a heart-
shaped raspberry cake for Valentine's
Day and even a cheeky clown cake
that children will love.

WHITE CHOCOLATE BOX

The discarded 'paper' cases in this pretty chocolate box are in fact made from white chocolate. The box also contains glistening gold and silver sugared almonds as well as white chocolate-dipped Brazil nuts and truffles, which make a delicious addition.

3-egg chocolate-flavoured Genoese Sponge mixture, see page 12
440g (14 oz/14 squares) white chocolate
470ml (¾pt/2 cups) double (heavy) cream
3 tbsp Amaretto liqueur
DECORATION
16 large Brazil nuts
10-12 truffles rolled in grated white chocolate, see Expert Advice right
12 silver sugared almonds
12 gold sugared almonds
1m (1 yd 3 in) gold- or silver-trimmed pink ribbon, about 1cm (½ in) wide

● Preheat oven to 180°C (350°F/Gas 4). Bake cake in base lined and greased 18cm (7 in) square cake tin (pan). Cool on a wire rack. Remove lining paper.

● Draw a 23 × 18.5cm (9 × 7¼ in) rectangle on a sheet of wax paper. Melt half the white chocolate, spoon it onto the paper and spread with a palette knife to just cover the marked rectangle. Shake paper to level chocolate, using the technique described on page 31. Leave on the flat surface until set.

● Melt the remaining white chocolate and use some of it to dip the Brazil nuts. Use the rest to make 12 chocolate petit four cases, following the technique on page 33. Leave to set.

● Using a long serrated knife, cut the cake horizontally in half. Place one half on a flat serving plate. Combine the cream and liqueur in a bowl and whisk to soft peaks. Use to fill and cover the cake, as described in Step 1 on page 62.

● Trim the white chocolate rectangle to precisely 23 × 18.5cm (9 × 7¼ in), using a clean ruler and a sharp knife. Cut the rectangle into 4 equal panels, each measuring 5.75 × 18.4cm (2¼ × 7¼ in). Secure these around the sides of the cake, following instructions in Step 2 on page 62.

● Finally, decorate the cake and board, following steps 3-4 on page 62.

EXPERT ADVICE

To make truffles, break up 125g (4 oz/4 squares) milk (German sweet) chocolate into small pieces and place in a small heavy-bottomed saucepan. Add 3 tbsp double (heavy) cream and heat gently, stirring until chocolate has melted. Remove the pan from heat and beat in 1 tbsp brandy, rum or orange-flavoured liqueur and 60g (2 oz/⅓ cup) icing (confectioners') sugar so that mixture begins to thicken. Cool. Using a small teaspoon shape chocolate mixture into small balls, then with your fingers gently coat in finely grated white chocolate.

continued from page 60

1 Spread about a third of the whipped cream over the cake. Gently rest second half on top. Use a palette knife to spread more cream thickly over sides of cake. Spread remaining cream over the top, smoothing it lightly.

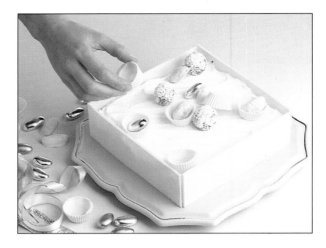

3 Scatter most of the chocolate-coated Brazil nuts, truffles and chocolate cases over top of cake. Arrange silver and gold sugared almonds over the chocolate decorations in an apparently random but neat arrangement.

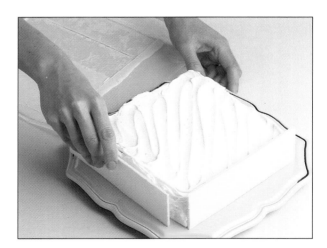

2 Carefully peel wax paper away from the chocolate panels. Place one panel against the side of cake and press gently into place. Complete box effect by fixing remaining panels in place so that edges meet neatly at all four of the corners.

4 Scatter remaining truffles, cases and nuts beside cake on plate or board. Tie ribbon neatly around cake, securing it with a dot of melted chocolate. Keep cake cool; it is best served the same day.

CHEQUERED CHOCOLATE PARCEL

Illustrated on page 65

Everything on this cake is edible, even the ribbon! Allow plenty of time for the decoration.

✦

60g (2 oz/⅓ cup) plain (semisweet) chocolate chips (bits)
Madeira Cake mixture, see page 15
1 quantity Basic Buttercream, see page 21
125g (4 oz/4 squares) plain (semisweet) chocolate
125g (4 oz/4 squares) white chocolate
½ quantity Modelling Chocolate made with plain (semisweet) chocolate, see page 32
½ quantity Modelling Chocolate made with white chocolate, see page 32
icing (confectioners') sugar for dusting

✦

● Preheat oven to 160°C (325°F/Gas 3). Beat chocolate chips (bits) into cake mixture. Bake in a base-lined and greased 1 kg (2 lb) loaf tin (pan) for 1¼-1½ hours until a skewer inserted into the centre comes out clean. Cool on a wire rack. Remove lining paper. Trim cake if necessary, see Expert Advice right. Cover with buttercream, following instructions in Step 1 on page 64.

● Melt plain (semisweet) and white chocolate in separate bowls. Spread on separate sheets of wax paper as described on page 31. Leave to set. Use to create the chequered effect on the cake, following steps 2-3 on page 64. Leftover chocolate squares can be used to make boxes, see page 31 if liked.

● Lightly knead both pieces of modelling chocolate. On a surface dusted with icing (confectioners') sugar, thinly roll each to a long strip. Using a sharp knife cut out thin strips from both colours, each about 5mm (¼ in) wide. Lightly dampen edges of a white strip with a fine paintbrush dipped in water; sandwich between two dark strips to make a striped ribbon. Press strips together firmly. Use remaining modelling icing to make more chocolate ribbon in the same way.

● Measure the distance from centre of top of cake to base on each side. Cut four strips of striped chocolate ribbon of appropriate length. For bow, cut two 13cm (5 in) lengths of chocolate ribbon and pinch ends together to make loops. Cut two shorter lengths for ribbon ends, pinching one end of each together and cutting out a 'V' from opposite ends. Finally, secure chocolate ribbon to parcel, following Step 4 on page 64.

✦ ✦ ✦ ✦ ✦ ✦ ✦ ✦

EXPERT ADVICE

The cake will probably 'dome' in the centre during baking. Slice top level once cake has cooled to create the parcel shape. A square tin (pan) could be used for a parcel of a different shape. For a novelty parcel cover cake completely with plain (semisweet) chocolate and use fancy cutters to shape animal, star or crescent white chocolate cutouts for securing to cake. Modelling chocolate will keep in a cool place for several weeks if tightly wrapped in a polythene bag. Break off pieces as required, kneading them lightly until pliable.

✦ ✦ ✦ ✦ ✦ ✦ ✦ ✦

continued from page 63

1 Using a palette knife completely cover cake with buttercream, making buttercream coating slightly thicker at top of sloping sides to give as square a shape as possible. Smooth down gently.

3 Using appropriate panels for each cake side, peel off squares as required and secure to cake in chequered design, making sure squares line up and fit neatly along edges. Continue design until all sides of the cake are completely covered in chocolate squares.

2 Cut out a panel from dark chocolate, exactly the same size as one long side of the cake. Cut the same from the white chocolate. Repeat this process for remaining long side, both ends and top of cake. Cut all panels into even-sized squares.

4 Position the four prepared lengths of modelling chocolate ribbon so that they meet on top of the cake, brushing ends lightly with water to seal. Fix bow loops in position and add ends. Neaten centre of bow with a small piece of ribbon.

CHOCOLATE HEART

Flavoured with liqueur and decorated with chocolate leaves and luxurious candied fruits, this cake is perfect for a special occasion. Fresh fruits may be used instead of candied, if preferred, but should only be added just before serving.

★

2-egg *Moist Rich Chocolate Cake mixture, see page 17*
4 tbsp brandy or orange-flavoured liqueur
COATING AND DECORATION
½ quantity *Apricot Glaze, see page 19*
500g (1 lb) *Marzipan (almond paste), see page 19*
icing (confectioners') sugar for dusting
315g (10 oz/10 squares) *plain (semisweet) chocolate*
125g (4 oz/4 squares) *milk (German sweet) chocolate, melted*
185g (6 oz) *mixed candied (glacé) fruit*

★

● Preheat oven to 160°C (325°F/Gas 3). Bake cake in base lined and greased 25cm (10 in) heart-shaped tin (pan) for about 1½ hours or until a skewer inserted into the centre comes out clean. Cool. Remove lining paper.
● Invert cake on a large flat serving plate or heart-shaped cake board. Drizzle with brandy or orange-flavoured liqueur.
● Brush apricot glaze over top and sides of cake. Roll out marzipan (almond paste) to a round, 30cm (12 in) in diameter, on a surface lightly dusted with icing (confectioners') sugar. Lift over cake and ease to fit around sides. Trim off excess marzipan around base of cake.

● Melt plain (semisweet) chocolate and spread over cake top and sides. Keep in a cool place until set.
● Melt milk (German sweet) chocolate, pipe a little from a paper piping bag with a medium writing tube (tip) following instructions below.
● Use remaining melted chocolate to half-dip fruits, see Expert Advice page 42, and to make about 8 chocolate rose leaves, see page 33. When chocolate has set, arrange fruit and leaves over top of cake.

★　★　★　★　★　★　★

EXPERT ADVICE

The Moist Rich Chocolate Cake should be baked immediately after mixing as soda is activated on being combined with liquid.

★　★　★　★　★　★　★

Holding piping bag about 5cm (2 in) above cake, pipe continuous fine lacy lines by moving your hand quickly over cake. To cover sides, tilt plate or board slightly with free hand and work with bag nearer surface of cake.

RASPBERRY VALENTINE CAKE

Fresh raspberries are used to flavour this special celebration cake, but other soft fruits such as strawberries, blackberries or blueberries would taste equally delicious.

★

6-egg Genoese Sponge mixture, see
page 12
125g (4 oz/1 cup) pistachio nuts, finely
chopped
ICING
4 tbsp Sugar Syrup, see page 25
125g (4 oz/¼ lb) fresh raspberries, sieved
into a purée
1 quantity Basic Buttercream see
page 21
1 quantity Glacé Icing, see page 25
30g (1 oz) Marzipan (almond paste), see
page 19
pink food colouring
icing (confectioners') sugar for
rolling out

★

● Preheat oven to 180°C (350°F/Gas 4). Bake cake in two heart-shaped tins (pans). Cool on a wire rack. Make several paper piping bags, following instructions on page 46.
● Warm sugar syrup and pour it into a small bowl. Gradually stir in raspberry purée, then chill mixture until it is thick enough to just coat the back of the spoon. Make up Basic Butter-cream in a large bowl. Set aside 1 tbsp of the thickened raspberry purée for piping; gradually beat the rest into the Basic Buttercream.
● Using one third of the Basic Buttercream, sandwich cakes together and then spread the

rest around the side of the cake, bringing it well up to the top edge to form a little ridge. Press the pistachio nuts over the side of the cake.
● Following the step-by-step instructions on page 70, ice the top of the cake and decorate with marzipan hearts.

★ ★ ★ ★ ★ ★ ★

EXPERT ADVICE

The feathering technique used to decorate this cake may be adapted for cakes of all shapes and sizes. Concentric circles of coloured icing piped onto white icing, dragged out from the centre with a skewer in alternate directions, look good on a round cake. On a square cake, the circles of coloured icing may be piped to radiate out from one side. When dragged, a fan effect is created.

★ ★ ★ ★ ★ ★ ★

continued from page 68

1 Put reserved raspberry purée in a piping bag. Make up the glacé icing and immediately pour it onto the cake, starting in the centre and working towards the edge. The icing should flow over the cake. Use the skewer to tease it into any awkward corners.

3 Quickly pull the top of the skewer across the cake in a straight line, through the coloured lines. Make a second drag line 1cm (½ in) from the first, but in the opposite direction. Continue making drag lines until feather pattern is complete as shown on page 69.

2 Snip the point off the end of the piping bag containing the raspberry purée. Pipe straight lines diagonally across the cake, 1cm (½ in) apart. The glacé icing should still be so soft that the purée sinks into it.

4 Colour the marzipan pink. Roll it out on a surface dusted with icing (confectioners') sugar to about 5mm (¼ in) thick. Cut out about 24 tiny hearts using an aspic cutter. Alternatively, make larger hearts, using a heart-shaped biscuit (cookie) cutter. Position round rim of cake.

EGGS IN A BASKET

Illustrated on page 73

To achieve a true egg shape for these chocolate eggs, melted chocolate is moulded inside thoroughly cleaned egg shells, which are then peeled from the hardened chocolate. The eggs are then dipped in melted chocolate and arranged in a basket-shaped chocolate cake for a perfect Easter treat. If time is short, bought chocolate eggs could be wrapped in the same delicate ribbon and used instead.

★

12 large eggs
500g (1 lb/16 squares) plain (semisweet) chocolate
500g (1 lb/16 squares) milk (German sweet) chocolate
500g (1 lb/16 squares) white chocolate
Madeira Cake mixture, see page 15
double quantity chocolate-flavoured Buttercream, see page 21
2m (2 yd 6 in) each of yellow, green and burgundy ribbon, about 5mm (¼ in) wide

★

● Start by making chocolate eggs. Using a clean skewer, carefully pierce a small hole in the thick end of one of the eggs. Break away a little of the shell to make a hole about 1cm (½ in) wide. Pierce yolk with skewer and pour contents out into a bowl. Repeat with remaining eggs.
● Thoroughly wash egg shells in warm soapy water taking great care not to break or crack any of the shells. Rinse, then leave overnight on absorbent kitchen paper to drain, pierced ends down (see Expert Advice, page 72).
● Next day, arrange eggs in a clean egg box, pierced ends up. In separate bowls, melt 375g (12 oz/12 squares) each of the plain (semisweet) chocolate, the milk (German sweet) chocolate and the white chocolate. Fill the eggs with the melted chocolate, following the instructions in Step 1, page 72.
● Make the Madeira cake. Preheat oven to 160°C (325°F/Gas 3). Grease and base-line a 3.4 litre (6 pt/15 cup) heatproof bowl with a circle of greaseproof paper (parchment). Spoon cake mixture into bowl and level surface. Bake the cake for 1½-1¾ hours or until a skewer inserted into the centre comes out clean. Leave cake to cool in bowl.
● Remove cake from bowl and trim domed top so it is level. Transfer to a cake board. Using a palette knife spread top and sides with half the buttercream, smoothing lightly.
● Place some of the remaining buttercream in a piping bag fitted with a writing tube (tip) and pipe basket, see Step 2, page 72.
● Remove chocolate-filled eggs from egg box. Roll them firmly on surface, then gently peel away shells to reveal chocolate eggs.
● Melt remaining chocolate in separate bowls. Roll a white chocolate egg in melted white chocolate. Lift out carefully between two forks, letting excess chocolate drip back into bowl. Place egg on a wire rack. Repeat with remaining eggs, dipping each in chocolate of the appropriate colour. Chill until set.
● Cut lengths of ribbon and use them to decorate the chocolate eggs, either tying the ribbons around them in bows or securing the ends with a little melted chocolate. Arrange eggs attractively in nest.

continued from page 71

EXPERT ADVICE

The processes involved in making this cake require a great deal of time to allow the cleaned egg shells to dry out and then the chocolate-filled eggs to set. Plan ahead and allow 2–3 days to finish the cake.

Don't be tempted to use a smaller bowl for baking the cake so that the bowl will be filled with the cake mixture. The wide, shallow shape is essential if the basket is to look authentic.

Don't waste the real eggs poured out from the shells. Use them in cakes or other dishes, but strain before use to remove any pieces of shell that may have fallen into the egg when the hole was being made. To make sure empty shells are thoroughly dry after cleaning, leave them overnight in the airing cupboard or in the oven once it has been turned off after cooking. If removing the shells from the hardened chocolate eggs proves difficult, place the eggs in the freezer for about 1 hour, then try again.

1 Spoon melted white chocolate into 4 shells, milk (German sweet) chocolate into 4 shells and plain (semisweet) chocolate into remaining shells. Leave in a cool place for several hours or overnight to harden.

2 Starting around top edge of cake, pipe short diagonal lengths of icing to create a rope work pattern. Pipe more rope bands under the first, working down to base of cake. Finish by piping a further rope band inside top rim.

EASTER NEST

Simnel cakes are traditionally made for Easter. This Madeira cake is less rich, but still has the layer of marzipan (almond paste).

★

Madeira Cake mixture, see page 15
almond essence (extract) to taste
125g (4 oz) Marzipan (almond paste), see page 19
icing (confectioners') sugar for rolling out
DECORATION
Apricot Glaze, warmed, see page 19
375g (12 oz) Marzipan (almond paste), see page 19
125g (4 oz/4 squares) cooking chocolate

★

● Preheat oven to 160°C (325°F/Gas 3). Grease and line a deep 20cm (8 in) round cake tin (pan). Add almond essence (extract) to cake mixture, then place half the mixture in the prepared tin (pan).

● On a clean surface dusted with icing (confectioners') sugar, roll out marzipan (almond paste) to a 20cm (8 in) round. Place on top of cake mixture in tin (pan). Carefully smooth remaining mixture over the top.

● Bake cake, covering top with greaseproof paper (parchment) if it begins to overbrown. When testing with a skewer, remember that centre will remain soft. Cool slightly before turning out on a wire rack.

● When cold, brush top and sides of cake with apricot glaze. Marzipan side of cake in two strips: Measure around cake with a piece of string and cut to size. Measure depth of cake in the same way, adding on 1cm (½ in).

● Using 250g (8 oz) of the marzipan, roll out two sausages, each half the length of the longer piece of string. Roll and trim each sausage shape to a strip slightly taller than the cake, using smaller length of string as a guide. Press the fine side of a grater firmly onto both marzipan strips to make a pattern. Holding cake on its side, roll it along one marzipan strip to fix it firmly in position. Repeat with second strip. Smooth the joins without spoiling the pattern.

● Roll out 60g (2 oz) of remaining marzipan into two strips to fit around cake. Twist strips together and fix on top of cake.

● Melt most of the chocolate (reserving a little for piping the eyes of the chicks) and make small caraque, see page 30. When dry, sprinkle over top of cake. Use remaining marzipan to make two chicks as described below.

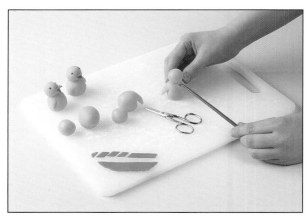

CHICKS

Colour a pea-sized piece of marzipan red and the remainder yellow. Cut the yellow piece in half to make two chicks. Roll a small ball for each head and a larger ball for each body. Assemble the chicks, then make a snip on either side of each chick for the wings. Cut two red diamond shapes for the beaks and insert into the heads. Pipe chocolate eyes.

SURPRISE PARCEL

This colourful gift-wrapped parcel cake is not all that it seems.

★

*4-egg Quick Mix Cake Mixture,
see page 10*
ICING AND DECORATION
*double quantity Basic Buttercream, see
page 21
juice of ½ lemon
Apricot Glaze, see page 19
wrapped sweets
double quantity Buttercream Paste,
see page 23
food colouring*

★

● Preheat oven to 180°C (350°F/Gas 4). Bake cake in a lined and greased 20 × 30cm (8 × 12 in) tin (pan), 25-30 minutes. Cool on a wire rack. Make buttercream, stir in lemon juice.

● Cut up, glaze and assemble cake as shown in step 1 opposite, using two thirds of the buttercream. Trim sides of cake to create a neat box shape. Measure sides and top of cake and make a thin cardboard template for each piece. Spread top and sides with remaining buttercream.

● The 'wrapping paper' is made from buttercream paste. Colour one eighth of the buttercream paste lilac and the rest a pale turquoise. Make panels, as shown in step 2 opposite. Assemble them around cake, box-fashion, smoothing joins neatly.

● Use remaining paste to make a label. Mark edges with a crimper or fork, leave to dry, then paint inscription. When dry, position on cake. Add a length of ribbon, as shown in illustration opposite, if liked.

1 Cut cake across width to make three pieces. Place two pieces on top of each other and cut a 5 × 10cm (2 × 4 in) hole through both. Brush with glaze. Sandwich layers with buttercream with holes on cake board. Place sweets in hole. Spread cake with buttercream; top with plain layer.

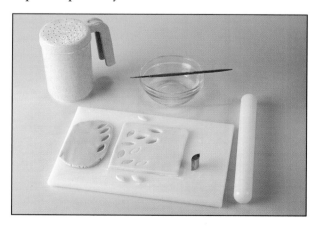

2 Roll out a piece of turquoise paste 5mm (¼ in) thick. Using template, cut out panels. Roll out a piece of lilac paste to the same thickness. Using cutter, cut shapes from both pieces. Dampen cut edges round holes in turquoise paste and insert lilac shapes. Seal.

CLOWN CAKE

A perfect cake for a small child's birthday. If you wish to add candles, press them into small balls of chocolate moulding icing. Attach them to the cake board.

★

double quantity of 3-egg Quick Mix Cake mixture, see page 10
200g (7 oz/7 squares) plain (semisweet) chocolate
ICING AND DECORATION
375g (12 oz) Marzipan (almond paste), see page 19
peach, yellow, blue, red and green food colouring
1 quantity Basic Buttercream, see page 21
1 quantity Chocolate Moulding Icing, see page 20
cornflour (cornstarch) for dusting
4 chocolate buttons
white chocolate chips (bits)
milk (German sweet) chocolate chips (bits)
1 liquorice 'bootlace'

★

● Preheat oven to 160°C (325°F/Gas 3). Grease two 1.1 litre (2 pt/5 cup) pudding basins and one 315ml (½ pt/1¼ cup) pudding basin. Base line basins with circles of greaseproof paper (parchment).
● Scrape cake mixture into basins and bake, allowing 35 minutes for small basin and 1 hour 10 minutes for large basins. Invert on wire racks to cool. Remove lining paper. Trim off top of cake baked in small basin to give rounded shape for clown's head.
● Melt plain (semisweet) chocolate and make chocolate case, following Steps 1-2 on pages 84-85. Colour half the marzipan (almond paste) peach and two-thirds of the rest yellow. Colour some of remaining piece red and some blue, leaving a small piece plain. Shape two thirds of yellow marzipan into two flat boots. Position towards front of cake board.
● Reserve 3 tbsp of the buttercream for piping. Using remaining buttercream, assemble large cakes in chocolate case, following Step 3, page 81 and referring to Expert Advice on page 80.
● Cut off one third of chocolate moulding icing. Reserve a small piece of this, about the size of a plum. Divide the rest in half for arms. Roll into thick sausage shapes on surface dusted with cornflour (cornstarch) tapering each 'sausage' at end. Flatten slightly, then bend for arms. Neatly cut off thin ends for cuffs, referring to Step 4 photograph on page 80 for precise shape.
● Still keeping plum-sized piece of moulding aside, use the rest to cover clown body, following instructions in Step 4, page 80. Secure arms in position using a dampened paintbrush. Use a cocktail stick (toothpick) to mark elbow creases. Press chocolate buttons into front of clown to make shirt buttons. Dot shirt with white chocolate chips (bits).
● Roll a little of the peach marzipan (almond paste) into two balls for hands. Flatten slightly, then cut 4 slits for fingers, using a sharp knife. (See Step 5 photograph, page 81 for precise shape.) Attach clown's left hand to shirt cuff.
● Roll out remaining marzipan to a circle about 18cm (7 in) in diameter. Wrap around reserved small pudding cake, easing paste and smoothing ends underneath. Secure to cake to form clown's head. Pipe hair, following Step 5, page 81.
● Shape reserved chocolate moulding icing

continued from page 78

into a small hat. Decorate hat with a liquorice 'bootlace' band and a small flower made from red and blue marzipan (almond paste). Fix hat on top of clown's head.

● Make braces, following Step 6, opposite. Roll out remaining yellow marzipan (almond paste) and cut out a wide collar. Position around clown's neck and finish with a blue marzipan bow tie. Shape mouth and nose from red marzipan. For eyes use plain marzipan rounds, pressing a milk (German sweet) chocolate chip (bit) in the centre of each.

● Finally cut remaining liquorice 'bootlace' into short lengths; press into boots for laces.

★　　★　　★　　★　　★　　★　　★

EXPERT ADVICE

When positioning the second basin cake to make the top half of the clown's body, place it towards back of the chocolate bowl so that it almost touches the bowl. This will leave a slight gap at the front emphasizing the 'baggy trousers' effect around the front.

When chocolate moulding icing is placed over cake the excess will fall in folds. Make sure these are at the back of the cake. Trim off any excess icing with a sharp knife, then gently smooth down icing, using hands dusted with cornflour (cornstarch) to remove creases.

The easiest way to pipe buttercream 'hair' is to begin with a few guidelines to frame face area, then fill in and build up with plenty of piped lines.

★　　★　　★　　★　　★　　★　　★

1 Cover outside of a 1.4 litre (2½ pt/6¼ cup) pudding basin with foil, tucking ends inside bowl and pressing creases as flat as possible. Melt chocolate and spread over foil to within 5mm (¼ in) of basin rim. Leave to set.

2 Carefully lift away foil tucked inside bowl. Twist bowl and remove it completely. With one hand gently resting in the base of the chocolate bowl, carefully peel away foil lining to leave a chocolate case.

3 Generously spread top of one large pudding basin cake with buttercream. Gently drop it into chocolate case. Position case on cake board, behind feet. Spread cake with buttercream; position second large cake.

5 Colour reserved buttercream green and place in a paper piping bag fitted with a writing tube (tip). Starting from top of head pipe vertical lines of buttercream hair, short at front for fringe and longer around neck.

4 On a surface dusted with cornflour (cornstarch), roll out remaining chocolate moulding icing to a 25cm (10 in) round. Lay it over top cake, tucking ends inside chocolate bowl. Ease icing to fit around back of clown.

6 Roll out two strips of blue marzipan (almond paste), each about 28cm (11 in) long and 5mm (¼ in) wide. Secure over clown's shoulders so ends just overhang trousers. Press chocolate chip (bit) into each end. Secure hand clutching brace.

WOODCUTTER'S COTTAGE

This chocolate variation on the familiar gingerbread house theme makes a good centrepiece for a special birthday tea. Position three bears – made from modelling chocolate – at the front door to recall the story of Goldilocks and the Three Bears. Although the cottage here is hollow, it could be filled with a chocolate sponge cake covered with buttercream to provide more servings.

⭐

315g (10 oz/2½ cups) plain (all-purpose) flour
60g (2 oz/½ cup) cocoa (unsweetened cocoa powder)
½ tsp baking powder
185g (6 oz) butter, softened
185g (6 oz/1 cup) soft dark brown sugar
2 tbsp black treacle (molasses or dark corn syrup)
2 eggs
DECORATION
250g (8 oz/8 squares) plain (semisweet) chocolate
125g (4 oz/4 squares) white chocolate
1 quantity chocolate-flavoured Buttercream, see page 21
30g (1 oz/1 square) milk (German sweet) chocolate
60g (2 oz) chocolate-flavoured Marzipan (almond paste), see page 19
4 large flaky chocolate bars (about ¾ cup shredded chocolate)
several chocolate buttons
icing (confectioners') sugar for dusting

● Make biscuit (cookie) dough. Sift flour, cocoa (unsweetened cocoa powder) and baking powder together. Beat butter and sugar together in a mixing bowl until just softened. Add treacle (molasses or dark corn syrup) and eggs with flour mixture. Mix to a soft dough. Knead lightly, wrap in greaseproof paper (parchment) and chill for about 30 minutes until firm.

● Trace cottage walls and roof on pages 92-94 on greaseproof paper (parchment). Cut out templates.

● Preheat oven to 190°C (375°F/Gas 5). Roll out some of the biscuit (cookie) dough on a lightly floured surface and lay it on a baking sheet. Cut out shapes, following Step 1 on page 89. Bake biscuit (cookie) shapes for about 10 minutes or until beginning to colour around edges. Remove from oven and leave on baking sheets for 5 minutes, then transfer to a wire rack to cool completely.

● Trace tree sections on page 91. You will need 5 tracings of large tree and 10 each of medium and small trees. On a separate piece of paper trace 12 window shutters and 1 door, using templates on page 92. Secure tracings to a flat surface with a smooth piece of wax paper on top. Melt plain (semisweet) chocolate in a heatproof bowl over a pan of simmering water. Place a little melted chocolate in a paper piping bag fitted with a writing tube (tip) and pipe over outlines of tracings, making sure joins are neat. Allow to cool and set. Place more melted chocolate in a bag fitted with a clean tube and fill outlines, easing chocolate into all the corners. Leave to set.

continued from page 82

● Melt white chocolate. Spoon a little of it onto the cottage walls. Spread with a palette knife, then make a swirled pattern over the chocolate with the tip of the knife. Repeat on remaining walls. Leave to set.

● Roughly spread a little of the buttercream over the surface of a 25cm (10 in) round cake board or flat plate to secure the cottage walls.

● Assemble cottage. Generously spread inner ends of each wall with buttercream. Carefully fix the four walls together, siting the cottage towards the back of the cake board or plate with the door facing the front. Gently position roof sections on the walls, following Step 2 opposite.

● Melt milk (German sweet) chocolate, put it in a piping bag fitted with a writing tube (tip) and pipe handles on the runout door and shutters. Shape a small chimney from chocolate-flavoured marzipan (almond paste). Complete the assembly of the roof, following Step 3 opposite.

● Place 3 tbsp of the remaining buttercream in a paper piping bag fitted with a writing tube (tip). Spread the rest of the buttercream over the board around the cottage, piling it up in patches to create a 'hilly' effect.

● Peel shutters and door away from paper. Pipe a little of the buttercream on the back of each shutter runout and fix them in place on the cottage. Finally add door, using buttercream to fix in position, and fixing it so that it is slightly ajar.

● Shape trees and attach to cake board, following Step 4 opposite. Make a path using chocolate buttons. Finally, using a fine sieve, sprinkle cake and board generously with icing (confectioners') sugar to give the appearance of fallen snow.

TEMPERING COUVERTURE

★

Couverture must be tempered before being used: Break up 500g (1 lb) couverture into small pieces. Melt it in a heatproof bowl over a pan of simmering water. When chocolate reaches 46°C (115°) on a sugar or chocolate thermometer, remove from the heat and place in a larger bowl of cold water. Stir chocolate until the temperature falls to 27-28°C (80-82°F). Return the bowl to the heat and heat to 31°C (88°F). The chocolate is now tempered and ready to be used.

★ ★ ★ ★ ★ ★ ★

EXPERT ADVICE

For a tiled roof effect omit the flaky chocolate bars and use chocolate buttons or even coloured sugar-coated chocolates instead. Chocolate runouts seldom break, but it is worth making a few extra tree and shutter runouts just in case!

★ ★ ★ ★ ★ ★ ★

1 Rest templates on biscuit (cookie) dough on baking sheet and cut around each, using a small sharp knife. Remember to cut out the window shapes and remove them. Lift away excess paste. You will need 2 roof shapes, 2 end walls and 1 of each long wall.

3 Carefully spread roof with buttercream and position chimney. Cut flaky chocolate bars into 2.5cm (1 in) pieces. Cut each lengthways into 3-4 flat sections. Starting from bottom of roof, secure sections in position with chocolate overlapping.

2 Generously spread the edges of one half of cottage roof with more buttercream. Gently rest one roof section in position so that point at top of walls is level with top of roof. Repeat on the other side.

4 Pipe several lines of buttercream up straight edge of one tree section. Holding this vertically, secure 4 more tree sections to the first, then transfer tree to buttercream-covered board. Make remaining trees in the same way.

CHRISTMAS WREATH

Chocolate leaves and tartan bows turn a simple ring cake into a wreath which would make an attractive centrepiece for a Christmas buffet table. An equally successful summertime version could be made using rose, lemon balm and mint leaves coated with pink or yellow coloured chocolate, and sugar flowerbuds.

✳

Chocolate Mousse Cake Mixture, see page 16
ICING AND DECORATION
*125g (4 oz/4 squares) white chocolate
green food colouring
60g (2 oz/2 squares) plain (semisweet) chocolate
60g (2 oz/2 squares) milk (German sweet) chocolate
60 rose, holly and bay leaves
1 quantity Chocolate Frosting, see page 28
1m (1 yd 3 in) green, red or tartan ribbon, about 1cm (1/2 in) wide*

✳

● Preheat oven to 180°C (350°F/Gas 4). Bake cake in base-lined and greased 1.1 litre (2 pt/5 cup) ring tin (pan) for 40 minutes until surface is crusty. Leave to cool in tin (pan), then loosen edges and invert onto a wire rack. Remove lining paper.

● Melt white chocolate. Following Expert Advice right, colour half of it pale green. Melt remaining chocolate in separate bowls. Use all the chocolate to make a selection of rose, holly and bay chocolate leaves, see page 33.

● Place chocolate ring on a large serving plate and spread with frosting. While frosting is still soft, decorate with prepared leaves, following instructions below.

● Finally cut ribbon into three equal lengths, tie into bows and position on cake. Keep cake in a cool place until ready to serve.

✳　✳　✳　✳　✳　✳　✳　✳

EXPERT ADVICE

White chocolate can easily be coloured in soft pastel shades to add interest to novelty cakes, leaves, cases, cutouts and runouts.
After melting the chocolate in a bowl over hot water, stir in a little oil-based paste food colouring, or powder. Do not use water-based colouring, the chocolate will thicken and spoil.

✳　✳　✳　✳　✳　✳　✳

Arrange prepared leaves attractively over cake, starting from outside edges and working towards centre. Try to arrange leaves in such a way that the different colours and types of leaf are evenly distributed.

CHESTNUT CREAM LOG

This may be served as an alternative to either Christmas pudding or the traditional rich cake.

★

2 quantities chocolate Swiss Roll mixture, see page 13
FILLING
1 quantity Crème Diplomate, see page 26
250g (8 oz/1 cup) unsweetened chestnut purée
30g (1 oz/2 tbsp) icing (confectioners') sugar
2 tbsp rum
DECORATION
1 quantity American Frosting, see page 27
½ quantity Basic Buttercream, coloured green, see page 21
45g (1½ oz) Marzipan (almond paste), see page 19

★

● Preheat oven to 220°C (425°F/Gas 7). Bake both cakes in lined and greased 20 × 30cm (8 × 12 in) Swiss roll tins (jelly roll pans). Roll up one of the chocolate cakes from the long side, see pages 12-13. Roll the other cake in the same way but over a rolling pin covered with greaseproof paper (parchment). Make several paper piping bags, see page 46.
● Make up the crème diplomate. Beat the chestnut purée, sugar and rum together and fold into the crème. Fill and roll the log, following the step-by-step instructions opposite. Chill for 30 minutes, as directed, then refer to the step-by-step instructions on page 90 for frosting and decorating. Keep the finished cake in a cool place and eat within two days.

1 Carefully unroll the thinner Swiss (jelly) roll. Spread half the chestnut cream over it. Roll the cake up again and hold it for a few seconds with the join underneath so that the shape sets. Spread the outside of the roll with remaining chestnut cream.

2 Unroll the Swiss (jelly) roll from around the rolling pin and wrap it around the first roll, tucking the join underneath. Wrap the cake in greaseproof paper (parchment) and chill for 30 minutes until set. To decorate, see page 90.

continued from page 88

3 Having filled and rolled log, see page 88, make American frosting. Unwrap log, place on cake board and cover quickly with frosting; cover length of log first, then ends. As icing sets, swirl it with a warm dry palette knife.

5 For trees, cut marzipan (almond paste) into three equal pieces. Mould each to a cone. Spoon Basic Buttercream into a piping bag fitted with a small ribbon tube (tip). Pipe small Buttercream ribbons around each cone. Top each tree with an upright stand.

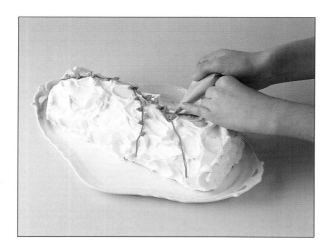

4 Place green Basic Buttercream in a paper piping bag, snip off end and pipe ivy stems over the cake. Fill a second bag with Basic Buttercream; snip end to 'V' shape and pipe ivy leaves on stems.

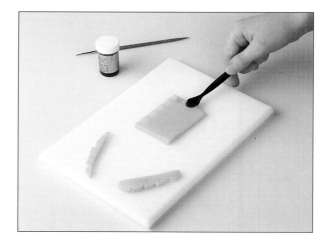

6 Roll remaining marzipan (almond paste) to a 5 × 7.5cm (2 × 3 in) rectangle and mark edges with fork or modelling tool. Pipe a greeting or design of leaves and berries, using the bag cut for piping the ivy stems.

TEMPLATES

Mocha Gâteau, *page 54*

Lace motifs

Woodcutter's cottage, *page 82*

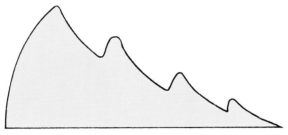

Small tree, make 10

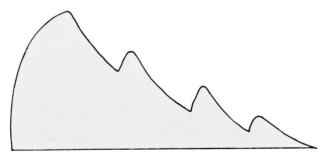

Medium tree, make 10

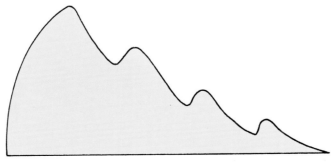

Large tree, make 5

Woodcutter's Cottage, *page 86*

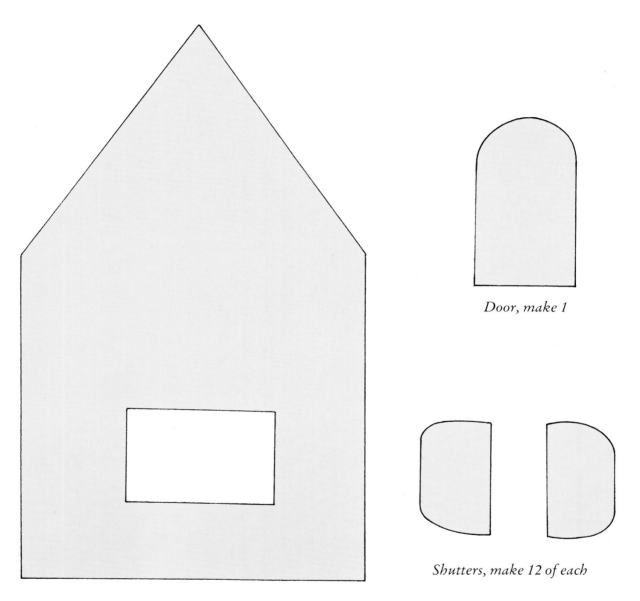

Door, make 1

Shutters, make 12 of each

End walls of cottage, make 2

Cottage roof, make 2

Cottage back wall, make 1   *Cottage front wall, make 1*

✦ GLOSSARY ✦

Beat/Cream A technique for mixing soft ingredients, usually with the intention of incorporating air. Using a strong wrist action, a wooden spoon is pushed through the mixture in a circular movement, trapping air when lifted. An electric mixer may be used.

Blend To gently mix ingredients together, either by stirring or by *folding in*, see below. Also used for processing ingredients in a blender.

Chill To cool food, either in the refrigerator or in a cool larder. Hot ingredients may be chilled quickly by placing the container in a bowl of ice cold water or ice cubes.

Coat To cover cakes with an outer coating of glaze, cream, icing or melted chocolate.

Cream See Beat.

Fold in To incorporate an ingredient into a lighter one without knocking out the air, as when sugar is added to whisked egg white. A large metal spoon is cut through the light mixture, which is then lifted up and folded over the heavier ingredient, using a figure-of-eight action. Care must be taken to scrape and lift the mixture from the base of the bowl, and to prevent the heavier ingredient from sinking and settling. Mixing should stop as soon as the heavier ingredient has been incorporated.

Fondant Traditional fondant icing is made by boiling sugar and then working the syrup into a paste. It is then warmed and thinned to be poured over cakes. Do not confuse with sugarpaste, which is sometimes referred to as fondant icing.

Frosting A cooked or partially cooked icing, originally comprising egg white and sugar syrup. Today more usually applied to a variety of cooked icings that can be smoothed or swirled and which dry to a crisp surface while remaining soft underneath.

Gâteau A light sponge cake sandwiched and decorated with a rich light filling of cream, meringue, fruit or enriched icing.

Genoese A light sponge, enriched by melted butter, made by the whisking method.

Glaze Literally 'to make shiny'. In sugarcraft the term is used when melted jam or jelly is applied to a cake to seal it and add flavour.

Grease To brush a tin (pan) or lining paper with melted vegetable fat (shortening) or oil to prevent ingredients sticking when cooked.

Knead This usually refers to heavy beating of a dough, but when used in connection with marzipan or icings, only a light pressure, applied by the fingertips, is required. The mixture is pulled out at one side and stretched before being pushed back on top of the main piece. The mixture is worked until smooth and pliable.

Nozzle See Tube.

Sieve A metal or nylon mesh utensil through which soft food is pushed in order to create a purée. Also used for dry ingredients such as flour, when the intention is to remove any lumps.

Sift To shake dry ingredients through a sieve or sifter to combine them to reduce the size of grains and to incorporate air. Ingredients should be sifted in small batches.

Slacken To make a substance – often a batter or icing – less stiff, usually by adding a liquid.

Syrup A sticky solution made by boiling sugar. Used to enrich icings, soften chocolate and thicken fruit purées.

Tube (tip) One of a range of small metal cones, each with a shaped aperture at one end. Placed at the end of a piping bag, it shapes the icing as it is forced through it. Also known as a nozzle.

INDEX